OVER WASHINGTON

HARALD SUND

THIS BOOK WAS MADE POSSIBLE
WITH THE HELP OF A GRANT FROM

SEAFIRST BANK
Expect excellence. MEMBER FDIC

OVER WASHINGTON

TEXT BY MURRAY MORGAN

PHOTOGRAPHY BY HARALD SUND

with additional photography by Georg Gerster

WELDON OWEN PUBLISHING
IN ASSOCIATION WITH KCTS, SEATTLE

HARALD SUND

HARALD SUND

WINGS OVER AMERICA®

This edition published in the United States of America
in 1995 by Weldon Owen Reference, Inc.;
820 Montgomery Street,
San Francisco, CA 94133. Phone (415) 291-0100,
Fax (415) 274-7383

Conceived and produced by Weldon Owen Reference, Inc.

ISBN 1-887451-01-3

WINGS OVER AMERICA® Series
Chairman: Kevin Weldon
President: John Owen
Associate Editor: Laurie Wertz
Copy Editor: Virginia Rich
Researcher/On-Site Location Coordinator: Barbara Roether
Design: Tom Morgan, Blue Design (from an original
    concept by John Bull, The Book Design Company)
Map: Mike Gorman
Production Director: Stephanie Sherman

Text by Murray Morgan
Photography by Harald Sund
Photographs by Georg Gerster appear on the
following pages: 156-7, 184, 185, 192-3, 194, 195
Principal fixed-wing pilot: Bob Southern
Principal helicopter pilot: Roger McKean
Publishing advisor: Vito Perillo

In association with KCTS
401 Mercer Street, Seattle, WA 98109, U.S.A.
President and CEO: Burnill Clark
Senior Vice-President: Walter Parsons
For the *Over Washington* television programs:
Executive Producer: Ron Rubin
Producer/Director and TV writer: Jeff Gentes
Videographer: Marc Pingry
Pilots: Rick Gerard, fixed-wing, Glen Bell, helicopter
Researcher: Sue McLaughlin
Historical consultant: Dan Peterson

Printed by Dai Nippon Printing Co., (Hong Kong) Ltd.
Production by Mandarin Offset, Hong Kong
Printed in Hong Kong

Distributed in the United States by
Pacific Pipeline, Inc.
8030 South 228th Street, Kent, WA 98032-3898

First published 1989, Reprinted 1990 (twice), 1991,
1992, 1995
Copyright © 1989 Weldon Owen Pty Limited
USA © 1990 Weldon Owen Inc.

Library of Congress Cataloging-in-Publication data:

Morgan, Murray Cromwell, 1916—
    Over Washington

    1. Washington (State) — Description and travel —
1981- 2. Washington (State) — Description and
travel — 1981- Views. 3. Washington (State) —
Aerial photographs. I. Sund, Harald, 1943-
II. Title.
F895 M58 1989   917.97'0022'2   88-33882

A WELDON OWEN/KCTS PRODUCTION

HARALD SUND

My sincere thanks to the principal pilots on this project
—Bob Southern ("King of the Wing"), Southern
Flying Service; and Roger McKean ("The Ace"), Classic
Helicopter Corporation—and to the many other aviators
with whom I have had the pleasure of flying over the past
years: Lee D. Roys, from Roys Surface and Air
Transportation, Inc. (my long-time friend); Frederick
Fager, Marty Weibel, Mike Everett, Mike Whittlesey, S.
Brent Davis from Classic Helicopter Corporation; Bill
Weber, Roger Black, Gene Glatt, Kirk Wheeler, from
Bergstrom Aircraft Inc.; Kathy and Steve Peters from
Spindrifter; Dave Driscoll from Corporate Aircraft
Services, Inc.; Dale Donaldson from DSD Enterprise; Jan
Liberty from The Ninety-Nines, Inc., International
Organization of Women Pilots; Andy Loesch, Tom Akers

from Wings Aloft; Mike Seager, The Aerie of Scappoose;
Bill Whitney, Kenmore Air Service.

Special thanks to those who have so generously
contributed their time and expertise to this project: Ken
De Jarlais, Chief Photographer, The Boeing Company;
Karen Walling, President, Meda C. McKean, Classic
Helicopter Corporation; Nanc Reznicek, Manager,
Sandra Johnson, Walla Walla Chamber of Commerce;
Ray Norton, Robin & Ray Advertising Specialties; Gary
Jennings, Gary's Bi-Plane; Rick Caldwell, Museum of
History and Industry; Richard H. Engeman, University of
Washington Special Collections; Floyd Lee Color Lab;
Naomi M. Anderson, Seafair; Truman Sheldon,
Okanogan National Forest.

— HARALD SUND

FOREWORD

Welcome to Washington state . . . an exciting place to discover. Our beautiful corner of the world has been explored by foot, horseback, bike, boat and car. After reading *Over Washington* you'll come away with another point of view—the view from above.

Soaring to new heights, Washington's geographical diversity and beauty is captured through aerial photography: from the rainforests of the Olympics to the basalt cliffs along the Columbia River; from the rolling hills of the Palouse to the 200-foot sea stacks of the rugged coastline; from the apple orchards of Eastern Washington to the glaciers of the Cascade Range.

World-renowned photographer Harald Sund returned to his home state to capture a new perspective of Washington, and together with historian Murray Morgan has produced a book which beautifully illustrates the state's development over a span of 100 years.

Over Washington celebrates the state's centennial along with KCTS/ Seattle, a leading PBS station serving the Northwest. Widely recognized for its commitment to providing excellence in local programming, KCTS produced an hour-long documentary and a series of short features that offer a breathtaking aerial tour of the Evergreen State.

Enjoy this book. It is a fascinating historical record of Washington, particularly significant as we celebrate our state's centennial.

BOOTH GARDNER
Governor, State of Washington

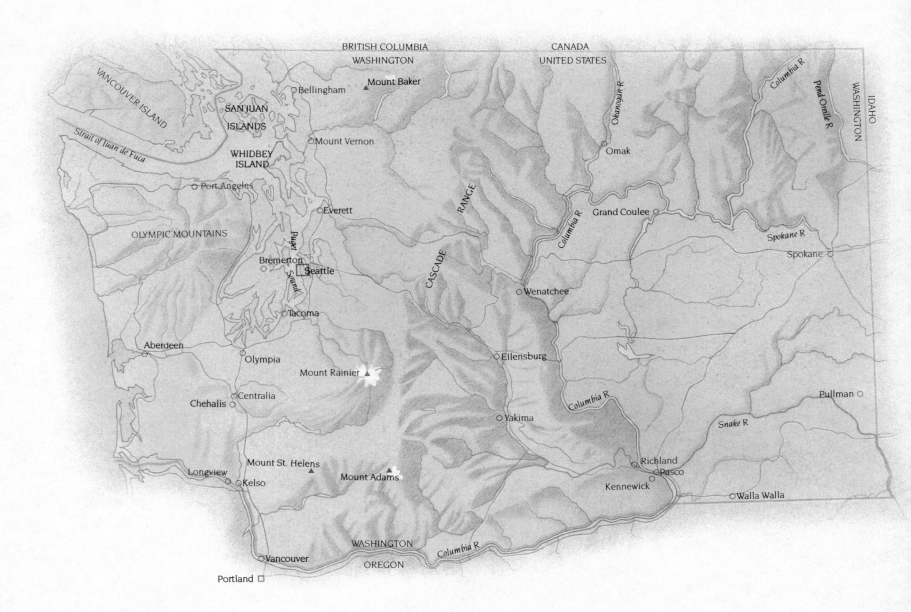

"I congratulate you, fellow-citizens, for the auspices under which our beautiful domain has been organized into a government of its own – the youngest of the American confederacy. The outpost of the great Northwest, looking on the Pacific and on the Hudson's Bay, having the elements of a great and varied development, commerce, manufactures, agriculture and the arts, it has received the name of the Father of his Country, and has had the impulse of its life at a great era of American progress and civilization – Its name, its geography, its magnificent waters are known throughout the land. The emigrant looks forward to it as his home; princely merchants as the highway of the trade of nations; statesmen and patriots as a grand element of national strength and national security."

(Territorial) Governor Isaac I. Stevens
to First Annual Session of Legislative Assembly
February 28, 1854

CONTENTS

Foreword by the Governor 9

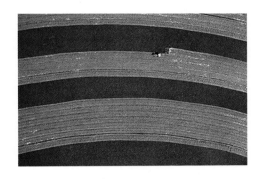

WESTERN WASHINGTON

Yachtsmen celebrate the continuity of
winds during Seattle's Seafair.

WESTERN WASHINGTON

*"I could not possibly believe that any
uncultivated country had ever been
discovered exhibiting so rich a picture."*

George Vancouver, 1792

Previous pages

The water remains the highway for the
San Juan Islands and Puget Sound.

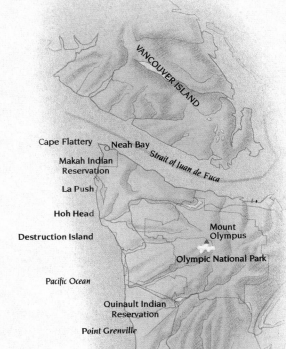

THE COAST

Late in the eighteenth century the clouds of mist and myth that shrouded the Northwest coast of America began to thin. The terra incognita that Jonathan Swift in *Gulliver's Travels* peopled with Brobdingnagians tall as church steeples; the "mapped imagination" that armchair cartographers in Europe laced with non-existent rivers and straits offering passage through America to the Atlantic; the never-never land on charts that Captain Cook cursed as "damned mischievous" yielded to reality. The yielding started in 1774. Spanish authorities, alarmed by dispatches from their ambassador to the court of Catherine the Great reporting Russian trading activity in the North Pacific, ordered that an expedition be sent from Mexico to determine whether the Russians had established settlements in America.

Juan Perez, the naval officer chosen to lead the expedition, was not to exploration born. A cautious type, accustomed to following established routes rather than pioneering new ones, he managed to sail the frigate *Santiago* from the mission in Monterey to the Queen Charlotte Islands off northern British Columbia and back to Monterey without once putting a party ashore to claim land. However, Perez did make the first confirmed sighting by a European of the Washington coast: a distant view of a snow-capped mountain range, the crowning peak of which he named Sierra Nevada de Santa Rosalia—now Mount Olympus.

The Viceroy, none too pleased with this performance, demoted Perez to second officer and sent the *Santiago* back north under the command of Bruno Hezeta. On its second trip the frigate was accompanied by the *Sonora*, a shallow-draft schooner, which, though only 33 feet long, carried 16 men under the command of a courtly young Peruvian, Juan Francisco de la Bodega y Quadra. On July 13, 1775, the two-vessel flotilla made a landfall near Point Grenville. The next morning Europeans first set foot on the Washington shore.

As light rain fell, a party from the *Santiago* staged a ceremony of possession. Watched by a few Indian boys who were cooking clams, marines paraded the beach, seamen moved rocks and cut brush to demonstrate control of the land, raised a cross carved with the inscription "Carlos III King of Spain by the Grace of God" and buried a bottle with a document claiming the land to be a possession of the crown of Castile. A few miles to the north a party of seven Spaniards went ashore from the *Sonora* to fill water casks. The Indians demonstrated their claim to the land by killing them all.

Hezeta was persuaded by his officers to press northward, but when the vessels were separated in a storm off Vancouver Island, he turned back south. Bodega y Quadra and his pilot, Francisco Mourelle, had determined to die in their tiny craft "rather than return without enlightenment." They pushed the little *Sonora* deep into the gulf of Alaska—to 58° 30′ north latitude—before turning back. It was the more cautious Hezeta, however, who brushed by an important discovery.

On the afternoon of August 17, an overcast day with strong winds from the southeast, the *Santiago* found itself off what appeared to be a large bay stretching toward the eastern horizon. "When midway between the capes," Hezeta noted in his diary, "I sounded in 24 brazas [132 feet]. The swirling currents were so swift that despite having a full press of sail it was difficult to get clear or separate myself from the cape to the extreme N., toward which the current tended to run . . . These currents and the seething of the waters led me to believe that it may be the mouth of some great river or some passage to another sea." Though he suspected that he was off the entrance to the long-sought Northwest Passage, Hezeta did not try to enter. Many of his crew were disabled by scurvy, and he feared they could not work the ship through the tumult of waves breaking on the bar. He dared not anchor to await better weather lest his men prove too weak to raise the anchor. He decided to stay off the bay during the night in the hope of calmer seas in the morning—a sensible decision but just one of a succession of sensible decisions by mariners of several nations that left the discovery of the Columbia River to a casual crossing of the bar by a Yankee trader in 1792, a feat that gave the United States its first claim to possession in the Pacific.

After Hezeta, the next European to pass along the coast was James Cook. The great English explorer was making a swift reconnaissance of Northwest America above the Spanish settlements while on his way to the Arctic for an attempt to sail around North America to the Atlantic. Arriving off the Oregon coast in March 1778, he encountered a series of gales that forced him to stay well out to sea. His first contact with the Washington shore was near the tip of the Olympic Peninsula. On March 22 Cook wrote in his journal: "There appeared to be a small opening that flattered us with the hopes of finding a harbour there." He charted it as Cape Flattery, a name it still bears, and noted "It is in the very latitude we were now in where geographers have placed the pretended *Strait of Juan de Fuca,* but we saw nothing like it, nor is there the least probability that iver any such thing exhisted."

During the night a gale blew in from the west. Cook's vessels hauled off shore, seeing no land for a week and missing the entrance to the waterway now called the Strait of Juan de Fuca (see pages 32-3). On March 31 Cook's ships put into Nootka Sound on the coast of Vancouver Island. There they stayed for four weeks while a new mast was fashioned for the *Resolution.*

The visit had important consequences. The sailors traded casually with the natives for furs, especially for the handsome pelts of the sea otter, the smallest but most richly coated of sea mammals. In China, on their way home from the Arctic, they learned that the Chinese placed an extraordinary value on the furs. The Manchu dynasty had mandated that robes worn at the imperial court in winter must be trimmed with sea otter. China had no sea otters, the Siberian herd had been overhunted, and the furs

North Head lighthouse on Cape Disappointment guards the approach to the Columbia River bar, called by one captain "the seven-fanged horror of the Pacific."

casually bought in North America and casually used aboard ship commanded an average price of $100 each, a princely sum. When the journals of the Cook expedition were published in 1784, they touched off a fur rush. Merchant vessels from several nations headed for Northwest America to trade with the Indians for sea otter skins. So began the commerce between the Northwest coast and the Orient, and Washington's trade relationship with the Pacific rim. Although mercantile in intent, the fur voyages added much to geographic knowledge of the coast.

The first commercial voyage from Chinese waters to the Pacific Northwest was made by James Hanna. He had come to Canton from India in the country trade—the shipment of cotton and opium from the Bay of Bengal—when he learned of the price commanded by sea otter pelts. On an investment of $4,500 he sailed to Nootka Sound and returned with skins that sold in Canton for $21,500. The word was out: there was soft gold to be found on the far side of the Pacific. But there was a problem: the East India Company held a government license for all British trade with China.

Charles William Barkley, a former officer with the East India Company, saw a loophole. He took his ship across the English Channel to Ostend in the Low Countries, registered it as Austrian and, with a 16-year-old English bride, sailed on the first commercial voyage from Europe to Northwest America. Coasting south after gathering furs at Nootka Sound, Barkley and his wife saw from the bridge of the *Imperial Eagle* a waterway stretching to the east. He noted it in his log but, a businessman not an explorer, did not enter. However, when he reached China to sell his furs, word leaked that he had sighted what might be the dreamed-of passage to the Atlantic.

John Meares, an imaginative, self-promoting rogue, was in China after a trading venture to Alaska. Obtaining access to Barkley's charts, he outfitted two vessels, registered them as Portuguese at Macao, and sailed for Northwest America. In a book published two years later he reported the existence of a waterway south of Nootka without mentioning Barkley. He also gave the name Olympus to the mountain Perez called Santa Rosalia. After visiting the capes that Hezeta speculated were at "the mouth of some great river or some passage to another sea" he declared "we can safely assert there is no such river." So he named the northern cape, Disappointment.

Before returning to China, Meares encountered at Nootka a one-eyed American captain, Robert Gray, who was to prove him wrong. Gray and another Boston captain, John Kendrick, spent the winter at Nootka. In the spring of 1789 two vessels belonging to Meares and his associates arrived. Next came a Spanish expedition, sent north from Mexico to garrison Nootka against an anticipated move south by the Russians. Instead of Slavs they found two American and two British vessels, the latter registered as Portuguese. Then more ships belonging to the Meares group showed up, this time under British colors. In the ensuing maelstrom of misapprehensions, Estevan Martinez, the Spanish commander, a hot-headed man, seized two British ships, imprisoned the crews, and sent the officers to Mexico to await trial for invading Spanish territory.

The resulting crisis threatened to start a general European war. Spain and England put fleets to sea and called on their allies for help. British Prime Minister Pitt eventually forced the Spanish to release the prisoners, return the ships, promise an indemnity (never paid) and sign a treaty that opened the Pacific Coast above the northernmost Spanish settlement (presumably San Francisco) to use by ships of all nations. Thus, the ebb of Spanish power in the Pacific began.

HARALD SUND

*B*eautiful and dangerous, waves swept across a quarter of
the globe strike the Washington coast.

*I*lwaco, cradled by the protective arm of Cape Disappointment, lives as it did in Indian times, off fish. Most of the early migrants were from Finland, and for several generations Ilwaco was as Finnish as the saunas in which the fishermen sweated away the fish smells.

*T*he merging of land, sea and mist is as difficult to decode today as when the Spanish approached Point Grenville in 1774 or when Wilkes nearly lost his ships on the Grenville Rocks in 1841.

*T*okeland, on the north side of the Willapa Harbor entrance, bears the name of an Indian chief famed for his skill in handling canoes in difficult waters. Today its lagoon, sheltered by a jetty, is harbor for a fleet of shrimp boats and crabbers, as well as charter craft for ocean salmon sportsmen.

A shrimp boat leaving Willapa Harbor.

HARALD SUND

HARALD SUND

Chehalis, a Salish word meaning "shining sands," was the Indian name for the river that reaches salt water between the twin cities of Aberdeen and Hoquiam, midway along the Washington coast. Hoquiam translates as "hungry for wood," which describes both towns. Built around lumber mills, the Grays Harbor ports continue to draw freighters for lumber products and, now, raw logs to be processed in Japan.

HARALD SUND

HARALD SUND

*N*o ships have been wrecked on Destruction Island, the mile long, 300-foot wide chunk of basalt 4 miles off the Olympic Peninsula. Its ominous name derives from the loss of two landing parties to Indian attack on the mainland. The Spanish lost a watering party near the mouth of the Taholah in 1775, the British a trading party off the *Imperial Eagle* in 1787. A Russian vessel was wrecked near the Hoh in 1804 and its crew held prisoner by the Indians until ransomed by a Boston trader. Men of the Lighthouse Service looked on duty at Destruction Island as tantamount to a prison sentence. The colony of horn-bill auklets, known as the poor man's penguins, offered some amusement but were so numerous that they were soon regarded as pests. The station was closed in the 1970s; the light is now automatic.

HARALD SUND

HARALD SUND

*H*alf-a-year's sail away from home, crowded into ships smaller than today's long-haul trucks, European sailors edged along this fog-enshrouded coast looking for openings dreamed up by cartographers who had never been to sea. Small wonder that Captain Cook cursed "those damned mischievous maps." *Left:* James Island looms in the foreground, the seastacks of Giant's Graveyard are obscured by the fog, and Hoh Head is in the distance. *Above:* The lovely curve of La Push, where gray whales pause to roll in the sand in early spring during their migration to the Arctic.

Following pages

*I*ndian legend has it that Portage Head, in the foreground, and Point of Arches, in the center, are the children of Destruction Island by his wife, Tatoosh Island. When Tatoosh ran away from her husband she threw them out of the canoe, saying, "You would probably grow up just like your father." Geologists say the formations are remnants of lava flows in the Eocene era.

HARALD SUND

Tatoosh Island, half a mile northwest of Cape Flattery, marks the entrance to the Strait of Juan de Fuca. Captain John Meares named it in honor of a chief whom he described as the surliest character he had ever met. Linguists disagree wildly about the translation of the name. Possibilities range from "breast" to "thunderbird." James Swan, who lived among the local Indians in the nineteenth century, said they never spoke of Tatoosh. They referred to the island as Chahdi, which translates simply as "island."

Cape Flattery lighthouse on Tatoosh, a brick tower rising from the roof of the lightkeeper's house, was completed in 1857. It was built in spite of objections by the Makah Indians, who used the island as their summer home. At first the light was fueled by lard oil, after 1885 by kerosene, and, since 1896, by electricity. It is visible for 19 miles.

HARALD SUND

HARALD SUND

THE LEGEND OF JUAN DE FUCA

In 1625 Samuel Purchas, an English collector of stories of geographic discovery, published a volume containing a letter he had received from Michael Lok, a widely travelled British barrister, some 20 years earlier. In it Lok told of meeting, in Venice in April 1596, an old Greek sailor who spun a marvellous tale.

Apostolos Valarionos told Lok that he had accumulated a small fortune while serving the Spanish as a pilot in the colonial empire, only to lose it all—60,000 ducats—in 1587 when the British privateer Thomas Cavendish captured the Manila galleon *Great Saint Anne* off Baja California.

Left destitute, he joined a Spanish expedition sent north from Acapulco to look for a water passage between the Pacific and Atlantic oceans. The expedition commander, a homosexual, had peculiar notions of the crew's duties. There was a mutiny, the ships turned back, the captain was convicted of sodomy and burned at the stake, and Valarionos was put in charge of a new expedition.

In 1602, after sailing to a point midway between 47 and 48 degrees latitude (mid-way on the Olympic Peninsula), he discerned a wide passage leading eastward. For twenty days he sailed through terrain "very fruitful, rich of gold, silver, pearl and other things" until he came to the "North Sea." Mission accomplished, he returned to New Spain to report the discovery of a Northwest Passage. The Viceroy thanked him but did not reward him. Neither did the King of Spain. So the old sailor was on his way back to Greece, but if Queen Elizabeth in her nobleness would return the 60,000 ducats he had lost to Cavendish he would be glad to guide the English through the Northwest Passage.

Valarionos added that the Spanish had trouble pronouncing his name and called him instead, Juan de Fuca.

The yarn attracted no attention when published. A century later it came to the attention of Arthur Dobbs, a wealthy Irishman with a passionate belief in the existence of a waterway across North America. He republished it. Thus revived, the Juan de Fuca story was noticed by Guillaume Delisle, a French mapmaker whose work was considered the most beautiful but not the most accurate in the world. Delisle inserted a Strait of Juan de Fuca on his next

map. Other cartographers followed his lead, placing the strait wherever it would add balance to conjectured coastlines. Captains who brought ships to Northwest America in the eighteenth century joined Captain Cook in cursing "those damned mischievous maps."

*L*ooking westward from inside the strait —Neah Bay and Cape Flattery on the American shore, Port Renfrew on the Canadian. Sailing ships often beat about these waters for days awaiting favorable winds to let them out into the Pacific.

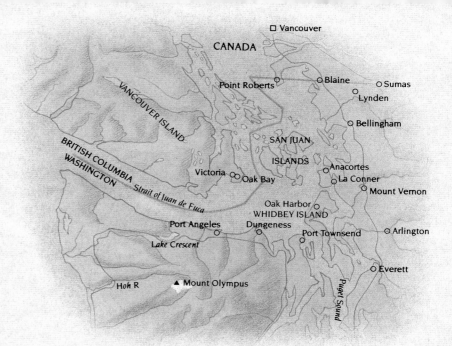

THE STRAIT

While diplomats in London and Madrid argued about the vessels Martinez had seized at Nootka, the Spaniards used one of them to explore the strait that Barkley had named for the mythical Juan de Fuca. In the spring of 1790 Lieutenant Manuel Quimper took the captured sloop *Princess Royal,* called by the Spanish *Princesa Real,* and sailed into the strait to see if it led to the Atlantic. He staged formal acts of possession on the north shore at today's Port San Juan, Sooke Inlet, Royal Roads and Esquimalt; then, the Indians having made gestures indicating that the strait ended in a large bay from which a broad channel led to the southwest, he crossed to the Washington side, finding anchorage in "a commodious harbor" (now Dungeness Bay), which he named for himself.

On July 8 Quimper claimed the bay for Spain. "Having armed the longboat and two canoes [I] embarked with the second pilot to take possession. This I effected, planting the Holy Cross close to a pine, on which another was made by cutting the bark. At the foot of this the bottle of possession was buried, all the ceremonies which the instructions prescribe being performed."

Second Pilot Juan Carrasco, sent eastward to see if there was an opening to the southwest, viewed from a distance the waters between Point Wilson and Whidbey Island. He decided they led nowhere. Quimper therefore charted what proved to be the entrance to Puget Sound as a shallow cove, Ensenada de Caamaño, honoring a fellow officer in the Nootka garrison. After charting Dungeness Bay (Bahia de Quimper) and Discovery Bay, which he named for Bodega y Quadra, Quimper returned to Nootka.

The following year, 1791, Lieutenant Juan Francisco de Eliza brought two vessels into the strait in another probe for the Northwest Passage. West of the bay that Quimper named for himself, Eliza entered a "much sheltered" harbor which he named for the saint on whose day it was discovered. Puerto de Nuestra Senora de Los Angeles is today's Port Angeles.

Eliza's attention was focussed on the north side of the strait, on the channels around the lovely scattering of islands he named the San Juans. Small boat expeditions went up the western passage that Quimper had named for his pilot, Lopez de Haro, and up the eastern passage that Eliza called Canal de Fidalgo, now called Rosario Strait. They emerged in what is now the Strait of Georgia and followed it to nearly 50 degrees latitude before lack of supplies forced them to return. "If there is anything of particular

From the east, looking down the southern end of Swinomish Slough to La Conner. Across Skagit Bay is the northern tip of Whidbey Island, then Saratoga Passage, central Whidbey, Admiralty Inlet and the Olympic Peninsula.

importance or consideration to be explored on this coast," Eliza said in his official report, "it is this large channel." He added that if this proved not to be a route to the Atlantic, there was none.

As for the possibility of a route south, Eliza elevated the entrance to Puget Sound from "ensenada" to "boca"—that is, from cove to bay. He did not attempt to enter it, explaining later that the Indians indicated it was too shallow for anything except canoes. Exploration of those waters could wait until next year or the year after. But next year brought another player on the scene: George Vancouver.

Captain Vancouver's assignment from the British Admiralty was to fill in the details of the chart of Northwest America sketched by Captain Cook. (Vancouver had accompanied Cook as a midshipman.) He was not looking for the Northwest Passage, the Admiralty no longer believing one existed, but he was to examine the Strait of Juan de Fuca to see if it was fed by a river that might provide a connection with the canoe routes established by British fur traders east of the Rockies.

Vancouver proved to be a poor hand at detecting rivers. He missed both the Columbia and the Fraser. Though, as he put it, he followed the coastline north from California "so minutely . . . that from the masthead the surf had been constantly seen to break on its shores" he declared flatly that the land "formed one compact, solid and nearly straight barrier against the sea." As for the Spanish charts postulating a river behind the foaming bar at the Bahia de la Asuncion, Vancouver agreed with Meares's name for the bay, Deception, and for the cape, Disappointment. He did not risk trying to cross the bar.

Nearing Cape Flattery, the English saw another sail—the first in eight months. It proved to be the *Columbia Rediviva* of Boston, commanded by Robert Gray, who had been on the coast previously in the *Lady Washington.*

In his book about his activities in the fur trade, Meares had said that Gray sailed the length of the Strait of Juan de Fuca, then went north, east and finally south of Nootka Sound, proving that Nootka was on a great island. Vancouver wanted to learn more. He sent Lieutenant Peter Puget and Archibald Menzies, the expedition scientist, to interview Gray on the *Columbia.* They returned to say Gray denied having made the trip. He had entered the strait but, finding little trade, turned back. Gray asked whether they had been able to get across the bar to the south, acknowledging that he had tried but failed. They expressed doubt that it marked the mouth of a river.

After the meeting, Gray followed Vancouver into the strait, apparently to make sure the British were explorers not rival traders. Then he turned south. Moving along the coast he noted an opening undetected by Vancouver or the earlier traders. He entered without trouble and found the trading good. During the night, however, Indians attempted to approach the *Columbia* in a manner that indicated an attack. "One large canoe with at least 20 men in her got within ½ pistol shot," the 19-year-old fifth mate noted in his journal. "With a nine-pounder loaded with langrage and about 10 muskets loaded with buckshot, we dashed her all to pieces." Trading resumed the next day.

On leaving Grays Harbor, as it is now known, the *Columbia* pressed south toward the bar that might or might not block the entrance to a river. Gray's journal is matter-of-fact about the most important maritime discovery by an American:

"Saw the entrance of our desired port . . . at 8 A.M. being a little to windward of the entrance of the harbor, bore away, and run in east-northeast, between the breakers, having from five to seven fathoms of water. When we were over the bar we found this to be a large river of fresh water, up which we steered. Many canoes came alongside. At 1 P.M. came to with the small bower in two fathoms, black and white sand . . . People employed pumping salt water out of our water casks, in order to fill with fresh, while the ship floats in. So ends." So ended the search for the great River of the West. Gray named it for his ship, the *Columbia.*

Meanwhile Vancouver's ships, *Discovery* and *Chatham,* had reached the head of the Strait of Juan de Fuca and found anchorage in the bay Quimper had named for Bodega y Quadra. Vancouver noticed stumps that seemed to have been cut with an axe. He surmised that other Europeans had been in the bay before him. That did not deter him from naming the bay for his ship, *Discovery.*

The Spanish, while in the bay, had shot an elk, the first killed by whites on the Olympic Peninsula. The British were not so lucky. Midshipman Thomas Manby shot a small animal "and was saluted by a discharge from him the most nauseous and fetid my sense of smelling ever experienced." Menzies, the scientist, was denied permission to bring the skunk aboard.

Vancouver and his crew spent 16 days in Discovery Bay. While the sturdy *Discovery* was being stowed with 20 tons of beach-gravel ballast to correct her balance, and the leaky *Chatham* (unaffectionately known as "our dung barge") was being caulked, Vancouver had the yawl, launch and cutter stowed with five days' supplies. Accompanied by Menzies, Lieutenants Peter Puget and James Johnstone, and a contingent of sailors, he set out "to become more intimately acquainted with the region in which we had so very unexpectedly arrived."

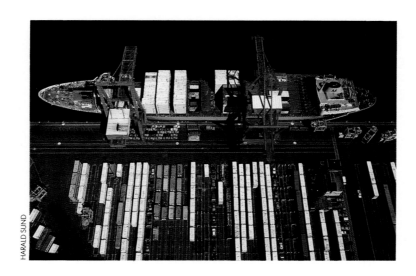

Container ships are the main carriers for the
two Pacific Rim ports.

HARALD SUND

HARALD SUND

*N*eah Bay remains the principal community of the Makah, a maritime tribe whose culture was, and still is, based on riches harvested from sea and shore. They hunted whales and seals from canoes, fished the depths for halibut, netted salmon during the spawning runs and gathered shellfish along the shore. Theirs was an economy of abundance. The sophistication of their numerous possessions was revealed when a perfectly preserved village, buried hundreds of years ago by a mud slide, was unearthed at Cape Alava. The Spanish established an outpost called Nunez Gaona, at Neah Bay in 1792, the first white settlement in the Pacific Northwest, but withdrew a year later. The Makah signed a treaty with the United States in 1855 that left them in possession of the northwestern tip of the United States.

Crescent Bay, 15 miles east of Neah Bay, is one of several shallow coves on the American side of the strait where attempts were made to establish a town. A wharf and warehouses were built but did little business. They were abandoned and later burned. A few residences are scattered along the curve.

Above

The forested hills behind the city fed the sawmills; Ediz Hook provided a sheltered harbor. Port Angeles grew as a mill town, then prospered as a tourist center and departure point for ferries to Victoria.

Port Angeles is the major port of the Olympic Peninsula. In 1862 Abraham Lincoln set aside 3,520 acres on the harbor for federal purposes, but the second national city that some envisioned failed to develop.

Following pages

Dungeness Spit, the extraordinary sandbar east of Port Angeles, was named by George Vancouver after a similar formation at the southernmost tip of Kent. The spit is now a wildfowl refuge and home to some of the world's most delicious crabs.

*H*urricane Ridge in the mountains behind Port Angeles is one of the most frequently visited areas in the 50-year-old Olympic National Park. During winter, snow lies 20 feet deep on the ridge but, by June, avalanche lilies are blooming at the edge of melting drifts. Summer brings a glorious conglomeration of subalpine wild flowers. Deer are common, elk herds sometimes seen. Jays are everywhere, scolding visitors who neglect to pay alms. In this picture, the visitor center is in the foreground. Behind the 5,200-foot ridge lies the valley of the Elwha. The Olympic Mountains bulk in the background, Mount Olympus slightly left of center.

Following pages

*M*ount Olympus is first among equals in the Olympic range. At 7,965 feet it is higher than its peers but does not dominate the splendid confusion of the interior peninsula. Here we see Olympus from the south in sunset glow. Above its crest can be seen the narrow strip of the Strait of Juan de Fuca which separates the Olympics from the mountains of British Columbia.

HARALD SUND

HARALD SUND

Crescent Lake, 8 miles long and 600 feet deep, was formed when a landslide blocked the Lyle River. Alternatively, as Indian legend explains the phenomenon, it was created by Storm King Mountain when he rolled boulders into the valley to create a barrier between the warring Clallam and Quileute Indians. The rain-laden winds off the Pacific encourage the growth of the evergreen carpet on the western slope.

Following pages

The valley of the Hoh shelters magnificent stands of old-growth spruce, fir and cedar as well as the tangled undergrowth of vine maple that distinguishes the temperate zone rain forest. William O. Douglas said, "This is not the place to run, to shout. This is a cathedral, draped in mosses and lichens and made of gigantic trees . . . They are among the great wonders of creation."

There are no bridges in the San Juan Islands. The water is both moat and link. Everybody has a boat, but the ferry is the workhorse, social center and old friend. Here a State of Washington ferry crosses Thatcher Pass.

Following pages

Sucia means "foul" or "dirty" in Spanish. Explorer Francisco de Eliza bestowed this name on one of the loveliest of the San Juans because its reefs made finding a good anchorage difficult without charts. A haven for smugglers during Prohibition, Sucia is now a State marine park beloved by boaters.

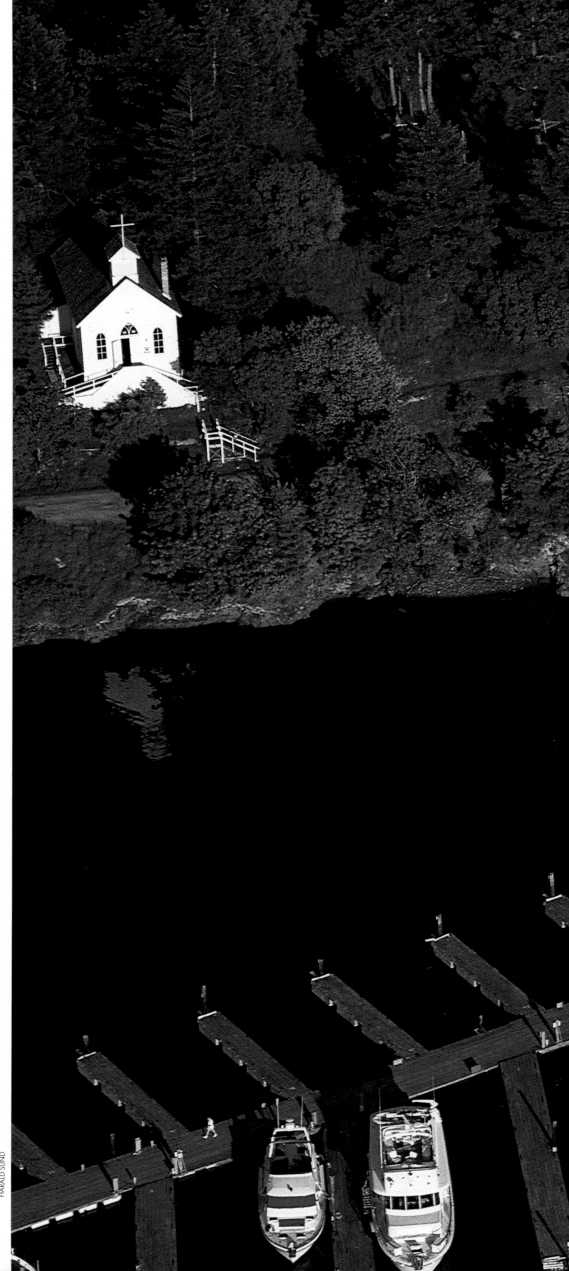

*R*oche Harbor on San Juan Island was developed as a lime quarry and personal barony by John S. Macmillan in the 1890s; a worker could be fired for not buying his shoes at the company store. The lime quarry has closed, but the charming old Hotel de Haro continues to enchant visitors as it did Theodore Roosevelt. A customshouse makes the harbor a calling point for large yachts. Our Lady of Good Voyage Chapel, on the bank to the left of the hotel, first served as a schoolhouse, was then used by Methodists for Sunday services, and, after standing vacant for several years, was consecrated as a Catholic chapel in 1960.

HARALD SUND

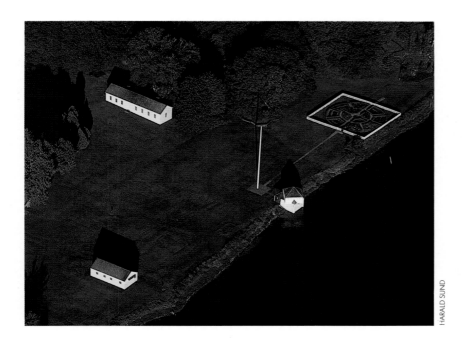

HARALD SUND

The Treaty of 1846, drawn up by diplomats who had never been in the San Juan Islands, stated that the boundary between British and American possessions should follow the "principal channel" through the archipelago. It did not specify whether Haro Strait or Rosario Strait was meant. Settlers made do without governance until an American farmer shot a pig rooting in his garden. The British owner of the pig obtained a warrant in Victoria for the arrest of the American, and asked the sheriff to enforce it. The commanding officer of American forces in the Pacific Northwest ordered troops to see that British law was not administered. The British responded with troops and ships. Moderates, however, won the day and years of delay. In 1872 the German Emperor was asked to arbitrate. He named Haro Strait as the boundary, giving the disputed islands to the United States. So ended the Pig War. *Above:* The restored buildings of the English camp. *Right:* American camp with False Bay in the background.

HARALD SUND

HARALD SUND

Top

Lew and Tib Dodd, a middle-aged couple from New England, bought Yellow Island in 1946. Together, they built a cabin, then a house from driftwood. They lived alone. After Lew's death in 1960 Tib stayed on for 20 years before selling her little Eden to the Nature Conservancy. *Above:* Lopez Island is the first to be visited by the ferry from Anacortes. *Right:* The northern tip of Lopez.

Following pages

Though on the mainland, Mount Baker is a presence everywhere in the San Juans. Vancouver named it for Third Lieutenant James Baker who sighted it on April 29, 1792. This view is from above the ferry landing on Shaw Island.

HARALD SUND

*E*ver since the Spanish-American War, the military has been a growth industry on Puget Sound. The nuclear carrier *Nimitz* approaches the Puget Sound Navy Yard in Bremerton. The Trident nuclear submarine base at Keyport is nearby.

PUGET SOUND

On the foggy morning of May 7, 1792, Captain Vancouver's flotilla of small boats rowed out of Discovery Bay, turned right and then rounded the northeastern tip of the Olympic Peninsula (which Vancouver named Point Wilson after a naval friend back home) and headed into waters unknown. When the fog lifted they found themselves looking down "a very spacious inlet" from which an arm forked westward. Far to the southeast they made out "a very remarkable high round mountain, covered with snow." The crowning peak of the Pacific Northwest received the name of Mount Rainier, honoring a somewhat obscure captain with whom Vancouver had served in the Channel Fleet in 1790. (Rainier, later a rear-admiral, had another claim to fame—he left his entire estate to help pay off the British national debt.)

When the longboats returned to Discovery Bay after eight days, they had charted Port Townsend (named for the Marquis Townshend, an eccentric cartoonist and antiquarian), and Hood Canal (originally named Hood's Channel for the Viscount Hood, who, as a member of the Board of Admiralty, had signed Vancouver's instructions and for whom Mount Hood in Oregon was later named).

Discovery and *Chatham* now being ready for service, Vancouver dispatched the tender under Lieutenant William Broughton on a reconnaissance of the San Juan Islands while he took the flagship south to continue the survey of the continental shore.

Anchoring at Restoration Point (named in honor of the anniversary of the restoration of Charles II to the throne in 1660) across the sound from Seattle, Vancouver dispatched two small boats under Lieutenant Puget to chart the continental shore southward. They returned in a week having proved that the inlet did not offer a passage into the Rocky Mountains but, instead, came to a dead end at what is now Olympia. Puget's report suggested names for several features in the southern sound—Dinner Point (now Point Fosdick) for the spot where they had their midday meal the first day out; Indian Cove (Wollochet Bay) commemorating their first meeting with the inhabitants; Crow Island (Raft Island) to note a breakfast of crows; Alarm Cove in memory of the expedition's only hostile encounter with Indians, a standoff over fishing rights that still has echoes; Long Island (Ketron Island); Wednesday Island (Anderson Island) and Friendly Inlet (Eld Inlet) for the southern reach where the Indians received them with ceremonial generosity.

Vancouver put none of Puget's proposed names on his official chart. Instead he called the southern extremity of the waterway—the portion south of the Tacoma Narrows—Puget's Sound. Vancouver's name for the whole area of British discovery—Admiralty Inlet—now denotes only the waters between Point Wilson and Seattle. Usage has bestowed on all the waters south of the strait the name Puget Sound.

With the return of Puget's party to Restoration Point, Vancouver crossed the sound and charted the eastern shore. On Monday, June 4, he marked the birthday of the reigning monarch, George III, by exceeding his written instructions and staging an act of possession, claiming the Pacific Coast from Cape Mendecino north to the Strait of Juan de Fuca, and all waterways connected to that strait, possessions of the Crown, to be known as New Georgia. After this, *Discovery* and *Chatham* sailed north, encountering in the vicinity of the Fraser River two Spanish vessels engaged in charting the waters east of what came to be called Vancouver Island.

What future did Vancouver and his officers see for the new-found land? They saw it through the eyes of men who came of age during the Industrial Revolution (Menzies, the scientist, was, at 38, the oldest man aboard). Steam engines were changing the pattern of life in Great Britain, but these men had no hint of a future that would bring this remote place not half a year's sail but half a day's flight from Europe; no way to know that horseless wagons would, within a century, cross the forbidding mountains to the east carrying hundreds of tons of grain bound for Great Britain on ships that sailed without sails; nor could they know that on waters within sight of Restoration Point would be launched a warship of metal, capable of destroying all the fleets of their day, and that in a nearby valley would be built a machine that would carry men over the roadless sands of the moon.

These men of 1792 thought instead of wooden ships and canvas sails. They saw on the shores "masts and spars for all the navies of the world," though Lieutenant Baker wrote that he was "of opinion that their remote situation from the Sea Coast render it most improbable that they will ever be of much use to Navigators," and Lieutenant Whidbey thought the area so distant that the best use for it would be as a depository for prisoners who had served their terms in the penal colony at Botany Bay.

Puget described Puget Sound as "most greatfull to the Eye . . . Nature, as if she studied the Convenience of Mankind, has so disposed of the Trees as to form on the Rising Grounds the most beautiful Lawns on which I have seen Grass [to] Man Height. Little would be the Labor in its Cultivation." Menzies was lyrical about the "salubrious and vivifying air impregnated with the balsamic fragrance of the surrounding Pinery." As for Vancouver, he declared that "the abundant fertility that unassisted nature puts forth, requires only to be enriched by the industry of man with villages, mansions, cottages and other buildings, to render it the most lovely country that can be imagined; whilst the labour of its inhabitants would be amply rewarded in the bounties which Nature seems ready to bestow on cultivation."

Settlers were slow to arrive. The Napoleonic Wars, growing out of the French Revolution, tied up British shipping. New England vessels dominated the mercantile trade with Northwest America until driven off the coast during the War of 1812, but they were interested in furs not farms. Some Yankee ships must have ventured into the sound, but few of the sea otters they hunted were to be found there. When settlement began, it came not through the migration of small farmers seeking to reap the bounties of cultivation but through a branch operation of an international corporation—the Hudson's Bay Company.

Penetration of the Pacific Northwest by land began early in the nineteenth century when traders of the North West Company of Canada found a path through the Rockies. The attempt by John Jacob Astor to compete in this transcontinental beaver trade collapsed during the War of 1812, leaving the North West Company dominant. It, in turn, was absorbed in 1821 by the Hudson's Bay Company, which was licensed by the Crown to monopolize the British fur trade in America and, west of the Rockies, to serve as a de facto government.

The Company established its western headquarters, Fort Vancouver, on the prairie on the north side of the Columbia, across from the mouth of the Willamette. Appalled at the expense of importing food (including salmon!) to the Columbia, Governor George Simpson of the Hudson's Bay Company decreed that posts must become self-sufficient. Soon Fort Vancouver had meat and grain to export. In 1833 the Company established a post, Nisqually House, beside Sequalitchew Creek on the prairie north of the Nisqually River. It was to serve as a trading post, a way station for the company's fur brigades moving between the Columbia and Fraser Rivers, and as a farm. The silty soil, deposited on the Nisqually prairie as the glaciers of the last ice age retreated, proved unsuitable for grain. Farther south the 15-inch loam on portions of the Cowlitz plain, yielded fine harvests so wheat was planted there, and the emphasis at Nisqually shifted to grazing livestock. The twin operations proved successful. The Hudson's Bay Company organized a subsidiary, known as the Puget's Sound Agricultural Company, to specialize in farming and ranching, and Governor Simpson negotiated an agreement with the Russian-American Company to supply its fur posts in Alaska with food. Yankee trading vessels had been supplementing their income from the fur trade by carrying supplies to the Russians; Simpson hoped that by depriving them of this revenue he could drive them out of the North Pacific. To a large extent he succeeded.

When the first United States government vessels—*Vincennes* and *Porpoise* of the Wilkes's expedition—arrived in Puget Sound in May 1841 (exactly 49 years after Vancouver) to chart the waters, the visitors were surprised to find Indian cowboys herding cattle, Scottish shepherds tending sheep, and the first steamship in the Pacific—the *Beaver* — riding at anchor off the mouth of the Sequalitchew.

There was a family of American missionaries at Nisqually, the Reverend John P. Richmond, his wife, America, and children including their son Francis, the first white child born on Puget Sound. At a celebration on July 5 (the Fourth fell on the Sabbath) Rev. Richmond gave the American eagle a lengthy flight, predicting "the advance of our dominion to the frozen regions of the north, and south to the narrow strip that separates us from the lower half of the American continent . . ."

Others present did not share his confidence. R. B. Robinson noted in his journal: "I am astonished that our Country should let them [the British] get such a secure footing as they already have got on this land."

Lieutenant Wilkes, the expedition commander, did his best to redress the balance, putting American names on every natural object, from rock to mountain that Vancouver had failed to name. Wilkes left on the map of western Washington a heritage of names that have become part of the vocabulary of everyday existence. It is almost impossible to go anywhere in the Puget Sound area without reference to his nomenclature. To him we owe islands such as Hartstene, Bainbridge, Maury, Fox,

Anderson, Henry and McNeil; bays such as Tacoma's Commencement Bay (for the start of one part of his survey) and Seattle's Elliott Bay; inlets named for the officers who led surveying parties, Eld, Budd, Case, Carr et al; and names on points and passages, and even rocks if they stuck out of the water.

This profusion of patriotic nomenclature had no effect when, five years later, diplomats drew the line that ended the joint occupation by Great Britain and the United States of all the country west of the Continental Divide, south of Russian America and north of Spanish America.

What proved to be decisive in bringing Great Britain to agree to a boundary following the 49th parallel to salt water was the Oregon Trail, the surge of American families along the wagon route from the Mississippi.

*F*ireboats help Seattle celebrate maritime festivals.

Opposite page

*P*ort Gamble on Hood Canal was the site of
the first mill built in Washington by two
Maine lumbermen, Andrew Pope and
Frederick Talbot. The town retains a New
England atmosphere and still makes boards out
of logs floated to the waiting saws.

HARALD SUND

*T*he State capitol complex, on a hill overlooking Budd Inlet, was designed in 1911 by architects under the influence of the City Beautiful Movement, which celebrated government through the use of classical antecedents. The self-supporting capitol dome, which rises 278 feet, is one of the highest in the world.

Previous pages

*B*remerton was chosen over Seattle in 1891 as the site for the Puget Sound Navy Yard. It has grown with each of America's wars—Spanish-American, World War I, World War II, Korea, Vietnam and the Cold War. Here the carrier *Nimitz* lies in the stream in front of the dockyard, dry docks and a fleet of mothballed vessels.

Following pages

*T*acoma on Commencement Bay bears the Indian name for Mount Rainier, the peak behind it. In 1889 the poet Joaquin Miller described this same scene: "Out of the blackness, above the smoke, above the touch of pollution, above the clouds, companioned forever with the stars, Mount Tacoma stands imperious and alone."

HARALD SUND

*S*turdy Gertie is the handsome successor to Galloping Gertie, which collapsed into the Tacoma Narrows only weeks after being opened to traffic in 1941. At 2,800 feet, Gertie's span is the fifth longest in the United States.

*T*he intricacies of Puget Sound below the Tacoma Narrows were charted in a week in 1792 by a longboat party under Peter Puget, but the maze can still puzzle those using it. From the bottom: Commencement Bay, Point Defiance, the Narrows with a bridge to Kitsap Peninsula, Hale Passage, Fox Island, Carr Inlet, McNeil Island, Pitt Passage, Longbranch Peninsula, Case Inlet, Hartstene Island, Peale Passage, Squaxin Island, Pickering Passage, Steamboat Rock, Totten Inlet.

HARALD SUND

The Seymour Conservatory in Wright Park near downtown Tacoma is one of the few surviving turn-of-the-century glass and steel greenhouses west of the Mississippi.

Stadium High School in Tacoma was originally intended by the Northern Pacific Railroad and the Tacoma Land Company to be the finest chateau-style hotel on the Pacific coast. After the project was abandoned during the financial panic of 1893, the city took over the building, completing it as a school.

HARALD SUND

*F*or many years Tacoma called itself the "lumber capital of the world." Its sawmills cut beams for New York subways, ties for Chinese railroads, shaft linings for Australian mines, boards to rebuild Tokyo after the 1923 earthquake, as well as the lumber for hundreds of thousands of American homes. But the old sawmills disappeared along with the first-growth timber. The lumber business of today is not the geometry of making rectangular boards out of round logs, but the alchemy of reconstituting wood into paper, cardboard, and fiberboard. Logs by the tens of thousands still find their way to Commencement Bay, but those that are not chipped into pulp are shipped whole to Japan where they are milled to dimensions not cut by American sawmills.

*T*acoma, the first city in the world to deliver residential power at a penny per kilowatt hour, twinkles in the twilight. The city expanded inland from Commencement Bay, its growth energized by low-cost power from dams outside the city limits—dams Tacoma had to win legal authority to build. The tideflats at the head of the bay are pierced by waterways dug by the Port of Tacoma to provide space for industry and warehousing. The long peninsula of Point Defiance, once set aside as a military reserve to deny hostile navies access to the southern sound, is now a city park, separated from the Kitsap Peninsula by the Tacoma Narrows. Olympia's suburbs shine behind the islands, and in the distance is the sunset glow off the Pacific.

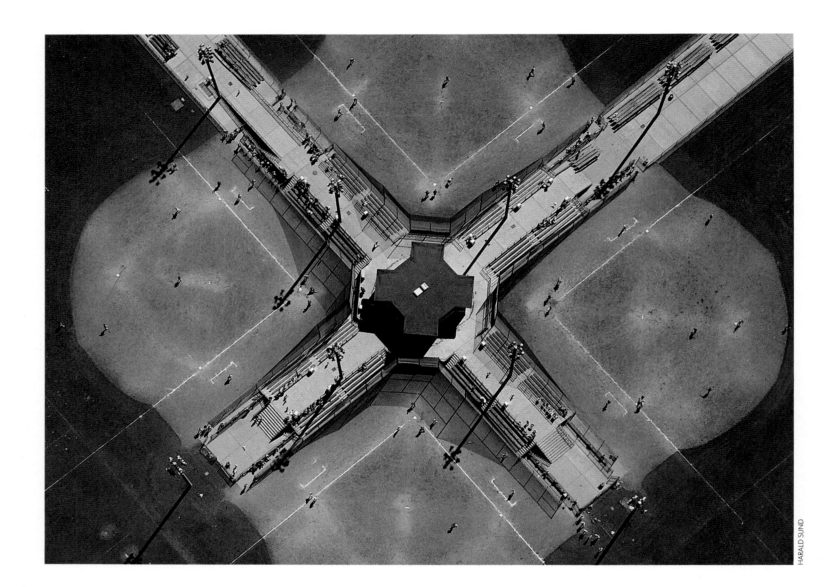

HARALD SUND

*I*n the White River valley between Auburn and Kent, not far from the scene of a massacre during the Indian War of 1855, four baseball fields await bloodless contests. The valley, once agricultural, is now increasingly devoted to warehousing and industrial plants, including the Boeing space center, where the moonwalker was developed.

HARALD SUND

An interchange on Interstate 5, near the headquarters of the Weyerhaeuser Company between Tacoma and Seattle.

Following pages

Federal Way gets its name from a school that, in turn, was named for Highway 99 running parallel to Interstate 5 between Tacoma and Seattle. It is one of the nation's fastest-growing unincorporated communities. Among its new facilities is the Wild Waves Water Park.

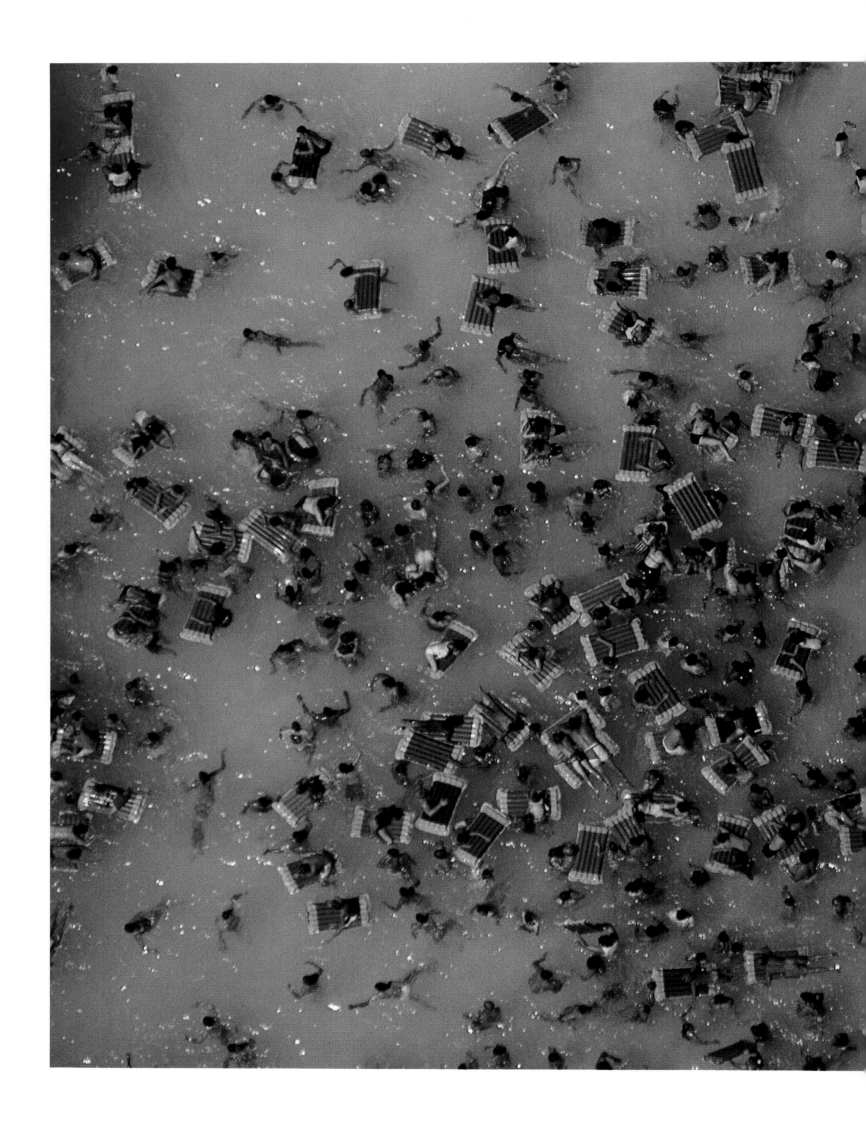

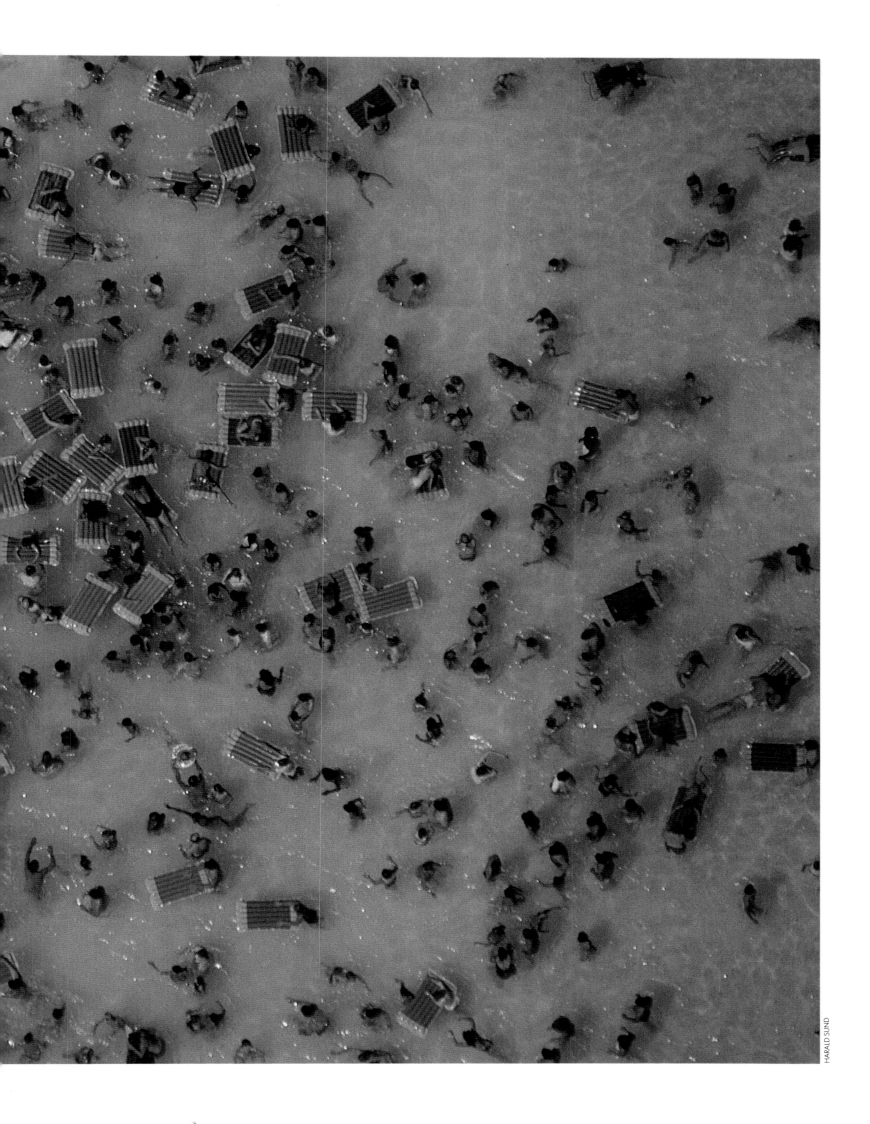

88

HARALD SUND

*H*ot air balloons rise from former hop fields near Kent as balloonists gather for the International Balloon Classic, held in conjunction with Seattle's Seafair every August.

*S*unbathers drying off, or simply displaying, create a mosaic at the Wild Waves Water Park.

HARALD SUND

A collection of vintage planes on the tarmac before Seattle's Museum of Flight. Among them, top, was a renovated B-29 Superfortress named Fifi, flown in for the occasion from an air museum in Harlington, Texas. Fifi represents the changes that World War II, and Boeing, brought to Seattle. In 1939 Boeing employed about 4,000 workers. A year after Germany invaded Poland, Boeing had 20,000 at work. In 1942, after President Roosevelt's call for the nation to produce 50,000 warplanes a year, Boeing's workforce reached 50,000. In 1944, production began on the B-29, the Superfortress, and sales for the year stood at $600 million. Seattle was booming, but would the boom last into peacetime?

*E*very day-and-a-half, a brand new Boeing 737 rolls out at the manufacturer's plant at Renton, south of Seattle. This 737-400 awaits a paint job to identify it with one of the more than 150 airlines who operate this aircraft type. By the end of 1989, Boeing had delivered nearly 1800 737s, but still had orders on the books for a further 900, making it the world's most popular jet transport. Boeing claims that nearly 2.5 billion people have flown in the 737 since its introduction in 1968 – the equivalent of nearly half the world's population.

HARALD SUND

*I*n September 1945, the month that Japan surrendered, the War Department terminated most of its orders for B-29s. Employment in Seattle's aircraft plants fell from 50,000 to 11,000 and Boeing's sales fell to 2 per cent of the wartime high. Boeing produced a civilian version of the propeller-driven B-29, which it called the Stratocruiser, and held its key workers and designers together until the Cold War in the Soviet Union and the "hot war" in Korea brought orders for jet bombers—the B-47s and later the B-52s. In 1952 Boeing turned to the production of commercial jet transports. It took seven years to apply the technology used for high altitude bombers to civilian transportation but the Boeing 707 changed the pattern of world travel and gave Seattle the right to call itself the "air capital of the world." *Left:* A building at the north end of Boeing's airfield has been painted with a checkerboard wall and striped roof to assist pilots on visual approaches to the landing strips. *Right:* A lineup of various models of Boeing's postwar jets.

HARALD SUND

*R*ide 'em, Aeromechanic! The Hat and
Boots gas station serves Boeing hands on
their way to the Ol' Lazy B.

*O*n the other side of town, Indians
assemble for a powwow and encampment
at Daybreak Star, the Native-American
art center in Discovery Park, overlooking
the waters they once called their own.

HARALD SUND

Seattle is encompassed by water; the sound on the west, Lake Washington to the east. *Above:* The serrated skyline of the business district forms a backdrop for yachts maneuvering in the annual Point Robinson race in May. *Right:* The shadow of Seattle's tallest building, Seafirst Columbia Center, lies across Lake Washington.

Previous pages

Seattle's central position on Puget Sound helped it to win control of shipping and eventual dominance of the regional economy. The days of the small boats—the mosquito fleet—are recalled during Maritime Week in May when tugboats race on Elliott Bay.

HARALD SUND

St. James Cathedral on Capitol Hill was built in 1907 and restructured in 1917 after the dome collapsed. On Memorial Day a huge flag fills the gap.

Right

*F*ramed by the sky-gray roof of the Kingdome and the cube shapes of its new neighbors, the Smith Tower reminds Seattle of its past.

*W*hen the 42-story Smith Tower was completed in 1915 it was the pride of Seattle — "the tallest building in the United States outside of New York, third highest mercantile building in the world." Overshadowed now by glassy neighbors, it retains its individuality and flies, by special permission of the city council, the salmon pennant of a previous owner and one of the town's favorite characters, the late restaurateur, Ivar Haglund.

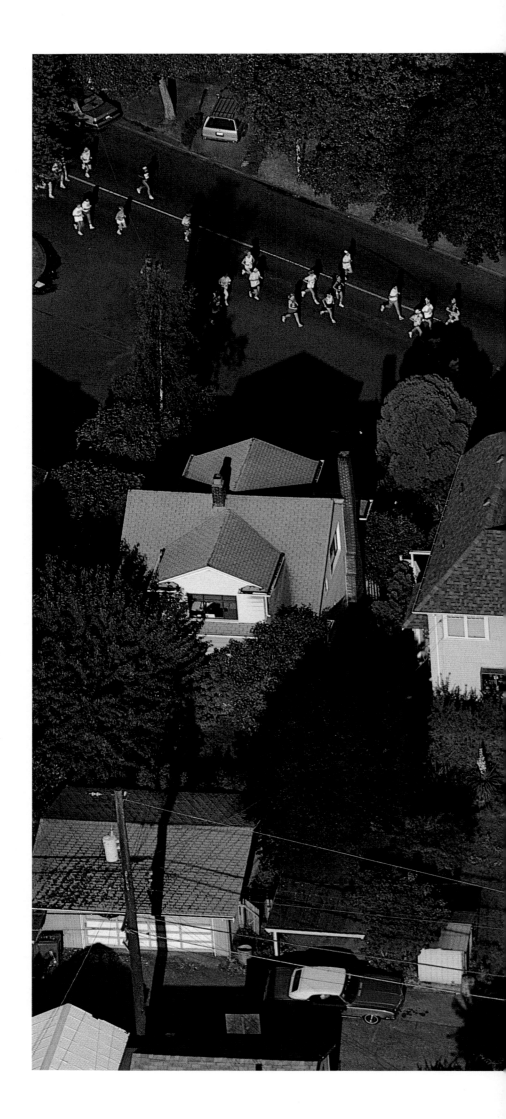

Neighborhood consciousness sometimes coalesces into city-wide opposition to projects conceived as primarily of benefit to downtown interests. More often, though, the neighborhoods celebrate their existence with events like the University District Street Fair or the Queen Anne Fun Run, shown here.

Previous pages

Although downtown Seattle increasingly resembles any big city with its highrise office space, canyoned streets, daytime congestion, and nighttime echoes, there remains in the rest of the city a strong sense of neighborhood. Areas like Rainier Valley, West Seattle, Laurelhurst, the University district, and Beacon Hill retain a pride in home ownership, an identification with their local high school, and an uneasiness that the city may become too big. Nowhere is the sense of neighborhood and community stronger than in Ballard, an enclave of Scandinavian workers annexed to the city in 1907.

HARALD SUND

HARALD SUND

HARALD SUND

*T*he University of Washington Medical School complex is named after Senator Warren G. Magnuson who shepherded appropriation requests through more than 20 sessions of Congress.

*T*he Convention Center astride Interstate 5 in downtown Seattle owes its existence—and its location— primarily to the influence of civic activist James R. Ellis.

HARALD SUND

HARALD SUND

The houseboat colony on Lake Union, once a haven for the romantic or indigent and now a nesting place for the young middle classes, was saved from rezoning and disappearance by the organizing skill of a much-admired former communist, the late Terry Pettus.

The mirror tower in Bellevue reflects the urbanization of the eastern shore of Lake Washington, made possible by the paving of part of the lake with two floating bridges.

*T*he 260-acre arboretum, seen here in spring finery, was obtained by the city from the Puget Mill company in a land swap in 1900. The arboretum is managed for the city by the University of Washington forestry department's Center for Urban Horticulture, which cultivates nearly every type of plant and shrub the climate will support. Civic activists have fought off many attempts at commercial intrusion.

HARALD SUND

When the Washington territorial legislature parceled out institutions with payrolls among the young communities of the territory in 1861, Olympia got the capitol, Port Townsend the customshouse, Walla Walla the penitentiary and Seattle, the clear winner, got the university. The downtown site of the first campus remains university property and a money maker. The university moved to its present site in 1895. In 1909 the campus was the site of the Alaska-Yukon-Pacific Exposition, which left a one million dollar heritage of landscaping by the Olmsted brothers and three permanent buildings. In 1915, President Henry Suzzalo and architect Carl Gould decided that upper campus buildings would be developed in Tudor Gothic style. *Left:* The cathedral-like library and the quadrangle remain the heart of the campus. *Right:* The Japanese cherries of the quad frame a favorite strolling area.

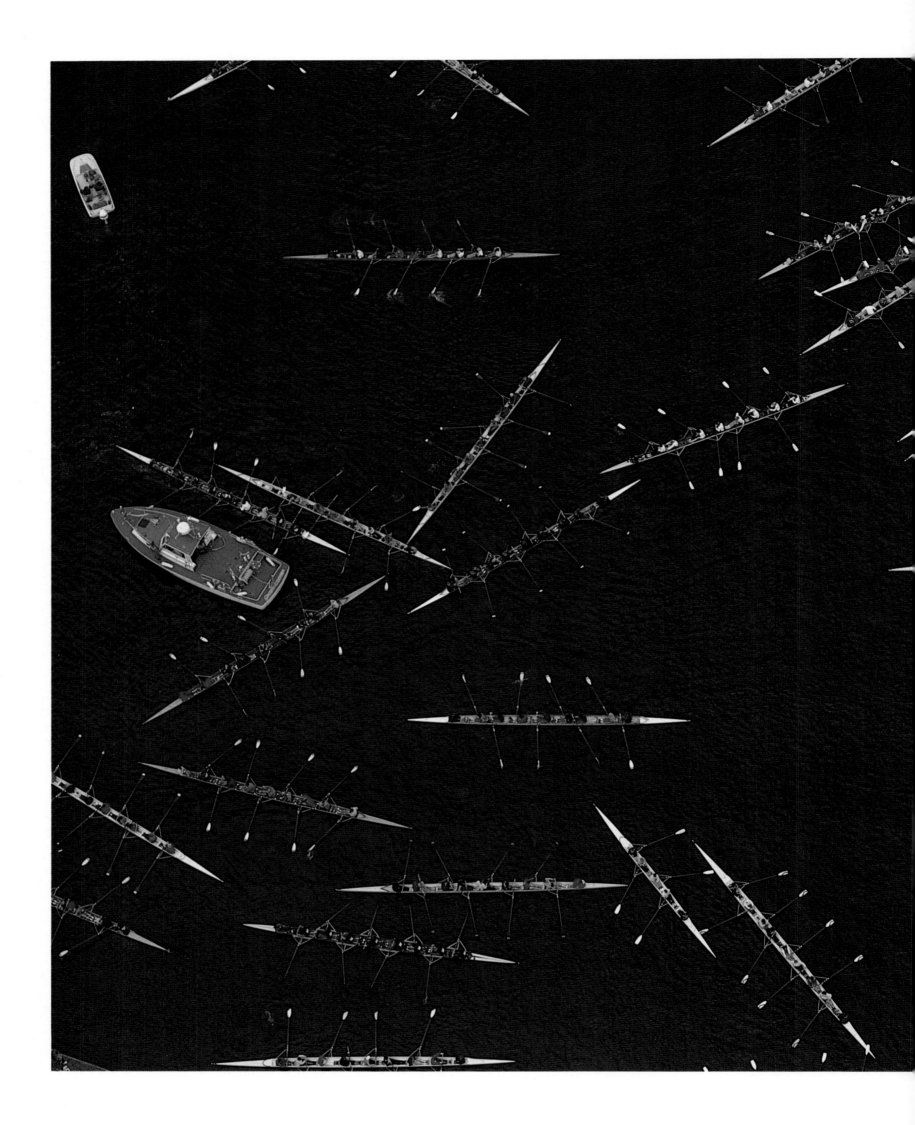

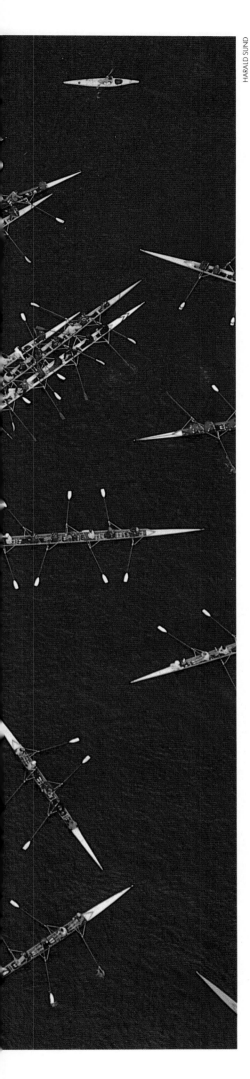

HARALD SUND

HARALD SUND

Water, water everywhere and some of it good to drink. Seattle has Elliott Bay as its frontyard, Lake Washington as its backyard, and a scattering of lakes, ponds, and fountains throughout the city. *Left:* On the opening day of the yachting season, racing shells assemble after the sprints through the Montlake Cut which connects Lake Union and Lake Washington. *Above:* Sailboats maneuver off the West Point lighthouse at the northern entrance to Elliott Bay. *Right:* Hydroplane races are a feature of the annual Seafair celebration. The Seattle-built *Slo-Mo-Shun* revolutionized the sport.

Following pages

Seattle boasts of having more boats per capita than any other American city. Here some boat owners get away from it all by huddling together for an aquatic tailgate party during the Seafair races.

HARALD SUND

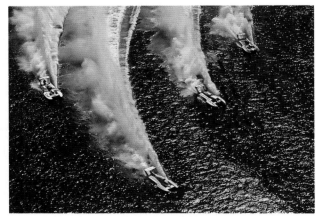

HARALD SUND

HARALD SUND

*F*ounded in 1907 as a place where farmers could sell their produce directly to consumers, the Pike Place Market has become one of Seattle's favorite institutions. When a proposed highrise development threatened to change the market's character, architect Victor Steinbrueck led a successful campaign to preserve it. Here, thousands assemble for the Pike Place Market Street Fair in May.

*S*eattle's dream of a waterway connecting Lake Washington, Lake Union, and Puget Sound was realized in 1916 with the completion of the Hiram Chittenden locks. These extended to 193 miles the freshwater frontage available to seagoing ships. The vision of a western Pittsburgh on Lake Washington gave way to the reality of desirable residential properties with waterfronts and a mountain view. Among visitors attracted to the locks in Ballard are not only yachts, freighters, and tourists but California sea lion bulls that come north in the spring to feast off salmon and steelhead passing through the fish ladders adjoining the locks.

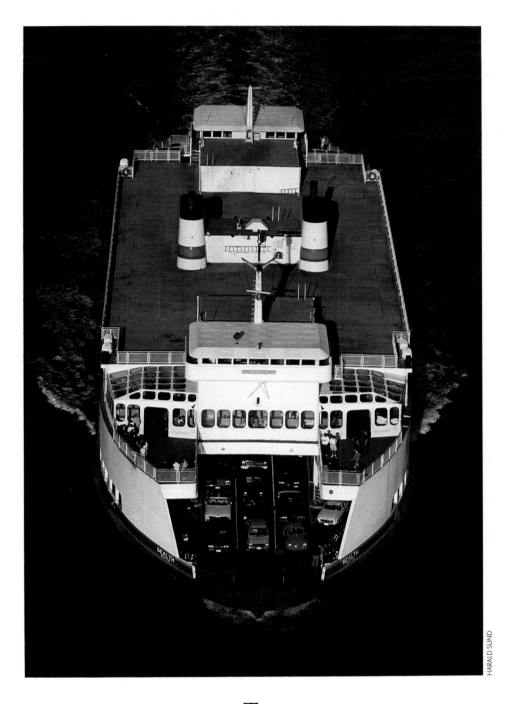

HARALD SUND

William Fraser Tolmie, the first white man to visit Alki Point, thought it would be a good site for a Hudson's Bay Company trading post "except for unproductive soil and an inconvenient supply of water." Seattle's first settlers, who landed at Alki Point on November 13, 1851, decided Tolmie was correct. They moved across the bay to a site more convenient for shipping.

The automobile ended the era of the mosquito fleet, the small boats that connected the cities of the sound. Islanders ceased to look on the water as their highway. Some considered it a moat protecting them against too much urbanization. But even a lord must sometimes leave his castle. Washington has the most extensive ferry system in the nation.

HARALD SUND

West Seattle was first connected to Seattle by viaduct and bridge in 1900. A second wooden bridge was built in 1910, a year after West Seattle was annexed to the city. Getting the bridges out of the way of boats remained a major problem until 1983, when completion of a high-elevation structure put an end to collisions and the complications of bridge raisings.

HARALD SUND

Seattle as it looks today from above the area where the Denny party landed in 1851. Brace Point is in the foreground and, behind it, the Fauntleroy ferry is entering Fauntleroy Cove.

HARALD SUND

At the time of the World's Fair, 1962, Prince Philip of Great Britain congratulated Seattle on its weather, "Let cats and lizards rejoice in basking in everlasting sunshine, but mists and drizzles and even occasional light rains make sunshine all the more welcome and constitute the proper environment of man. They prevent the dreaded dehydration which shrivels the brain, makes sluggish the blood and dims the moist and flashing eye." *Above:* Seattlites risk the sun on Lake Washington Boulevard during Seafair and (*right*) at Alki Beach on a Sunday.

HARALD SUND

The first settlers in Seattle anticipated that the community would prosper by controlling the trade from farms in the Duwamish–White River valley. David Denny predicted that there would be "room for 1,000 settlers" upriver. The major "crop" from the Duwamish valley today is jet transport. *Above:* Man-made Harbor Island at the river mouth produces ships. *Right:* Physician David "Doc" Maynard pioneered another Seattle industry when he put salmon in brine for shipment to San Francisco. The shipment spoiled, but the fishery remains important. Here fishing boats cluster around a cannery on Lake Union.

Previous pages

In 1950, Bellevue on the east side of Lake Washington claimed a population of about one thousand and was described in guide books as a trading center for berry farmers and the home port of the last six American whaling ships. With the building of the bridges, the east side expanded, eventually to become a friendly rival capable of competing with the Emerald City for new enterprises.

HARALD SUND

*F*rom the revolving restaurant, atop the
Space Needle, diners can watch shipping
move across Elliott Bay. Here a tug tows
a pair of massive barges toward Seattle
while, in the foreground, wheat from
eastern Washington is discharged from
the grain elevator into a container ship.
Right: From Hunts Point, on the eastern
shore of Lake Washington, the Space
Needle can be seen above Seattle's hills
with the sound and Olympic Mountains
in the distance. In the foreground, the
concrete Evergreen Point Bridge floats
on the lake.

HARALD SUND

HARALD SUND

*U*naided nature proved that western Washington was an ideal place to grow trees, but farmers have learned that the narrow valleys cup richer, deeper soil for vegetables and grain. *Above:* Alfalfa is being harvested in the Carnation Valley, home base for the Carnation Milk Products Company, a pioneer in the production of condensed milk. *Right:* A combine works in a field fitted into the forest. The brown carpet is wheat, the green strips are corn, the gray soil lies fallow.

HARALD SUND

A tanker discharges gasoline at a tank farm at Richmond Beach between Seattle and Everett.

*M*onroe, once a logging town but now the center of a rich agricultural area, plays host annually to the Evergreen State Fair.

HARALD SUND

The Washington State International Air Fair at Paine Field near Everett is one of the largest such exhibitions in the country.

On weekends, a drive-in movie lot near Everett takes on a carnival atmosphere as vendors and customers gather at a flea market.

HARALD SUND

HARALD SUND

*T*he men who founded Everett planned
an industrial town that would smelt
metals from the surrounding hills and
turn out steel ships. The ore was not
there. Lumber became the basic industry.
The Weyerhaeuser Company's first large
mill was built here.

*W*hen chemists discovered the sulfate
process for turning the chips from
hemlock spruce into pulp for paper they
transformed a weed tree, abundant on
Puget Sound, into an economic asset . . .
but an olfactory liability. What smells
like dollars to those who benefit from the
process, smells like rotten eggs to others.
But, seen from the air, the aeration
ponds used in the process have the
beauty of sea anemones.

136

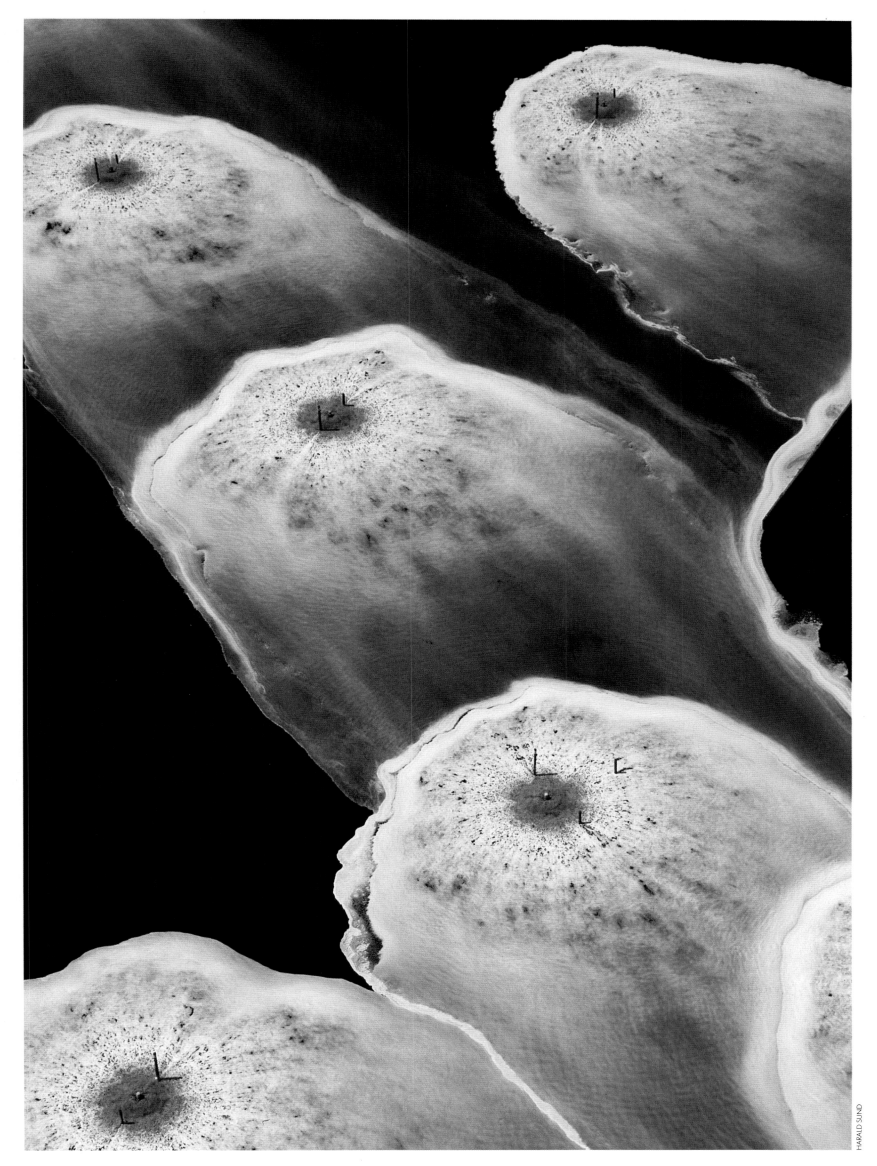

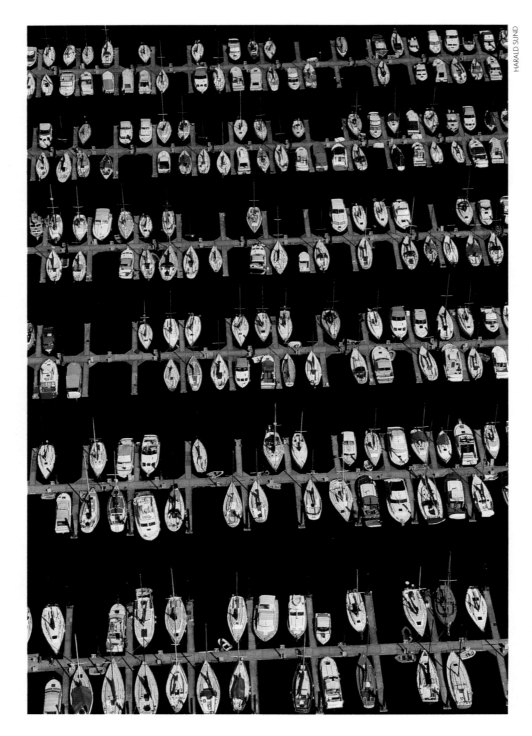

HARALD SUND

*Y*acht ownership is so prevalent among those who live by the inland sea that there is a mooring problem. Marinas are a thriving industry. This one is operated by the Port of Everett.

*D*erelict vessels were used to form a breakwater at the mouth of the Snohomish River around the turn of the century. Rafts of logs, sheltered behind it, await towing to the mills. After more than 60 years performing its humble guard duty, the hulk of the *Equator,* a yacht used by Robert Louis Stevenson during his Polynesian years, was discovered. It is now being restored.

HARALD SUND

Many Scandinavians were attracted to the lumber and farming area on the delta of the Stillaguamish River. They created this severe but beautiful Lutheran church at Silvana, near Arlington.

Deception Pass, which lies between Whidbey and Fidalgo islands, connecting Skagit Bay with the sound was so named because it seems to lead nowhere. It looks deceptively calm in this picture but the *United States Coast Pilot* warns that "currents in the narrows attain velocities of 5 to 8 knots, at which times strong eddies are formed along the shores."

HARALD SUND

HARALD SUND

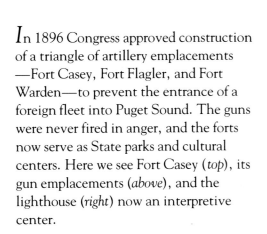

*I*n 1896 Congress approved construction of a triangle of artillery emplacements —Fort Casey, Fort Flagler, and Fort Warden—to prevent the entrance of a foreign fleet into Puget Sound. The guns were never fired in anger, and the forts now serve as State parks and cultural centers. Here we see Fort Casey (*top*), its gun emplacements (*above*), and the lighthouse (*right*) now an interpretive center.

HARALD SUND

Old-timers of the air and home-built craft, one fabricated by a teenager in her basement, fly into Arlington for an annual exhibition of the way it used to be.

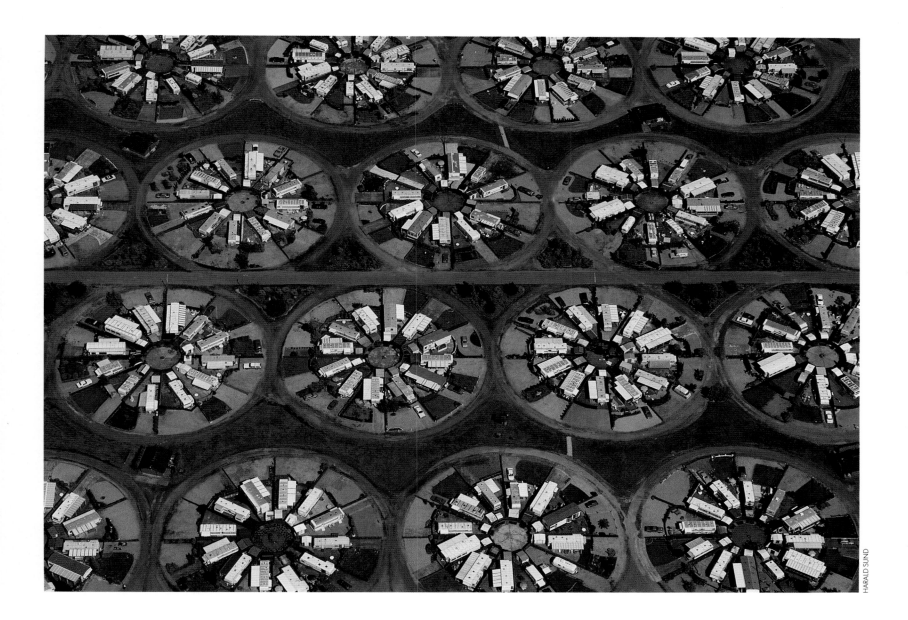

HARALD SUND

Mobile-home parks, not always
attractive when seen from the highway,
may have an odd beauty from above.
This one is near Birch Bay on the
Canadian border. It is a part of a growing
complex of retirement and recreational
developments that take advantage of the
short drive to Vancouver, British
Columbia, one of the most attractive
cities on the Pacific Coast.

HARALD SUND

Around 1900 a number of Dutch farmers, attracted by the rich bottom lands in the Nooksack valley, planted tulips and daffodils, turning the area into a Little Holland. When the market for bulbs became overcrowded they took up dairy farming. Although willing to change their farming ways, they cling to other traditions. Lynden still has a city ordinance prohibiting dancing.

The Skagit River delta, south of Mount Vernon, boasts some of Washington's most productive land. The tractor gives a sense of the size of these tulip fields in April bloom.

Following pages

Anacortes is the departure point for ferries to the San Juans and Vancouver Island. The jetties protect the terminal for an oil refinery. Guemes and Cypress islands loom against the fading sunset.

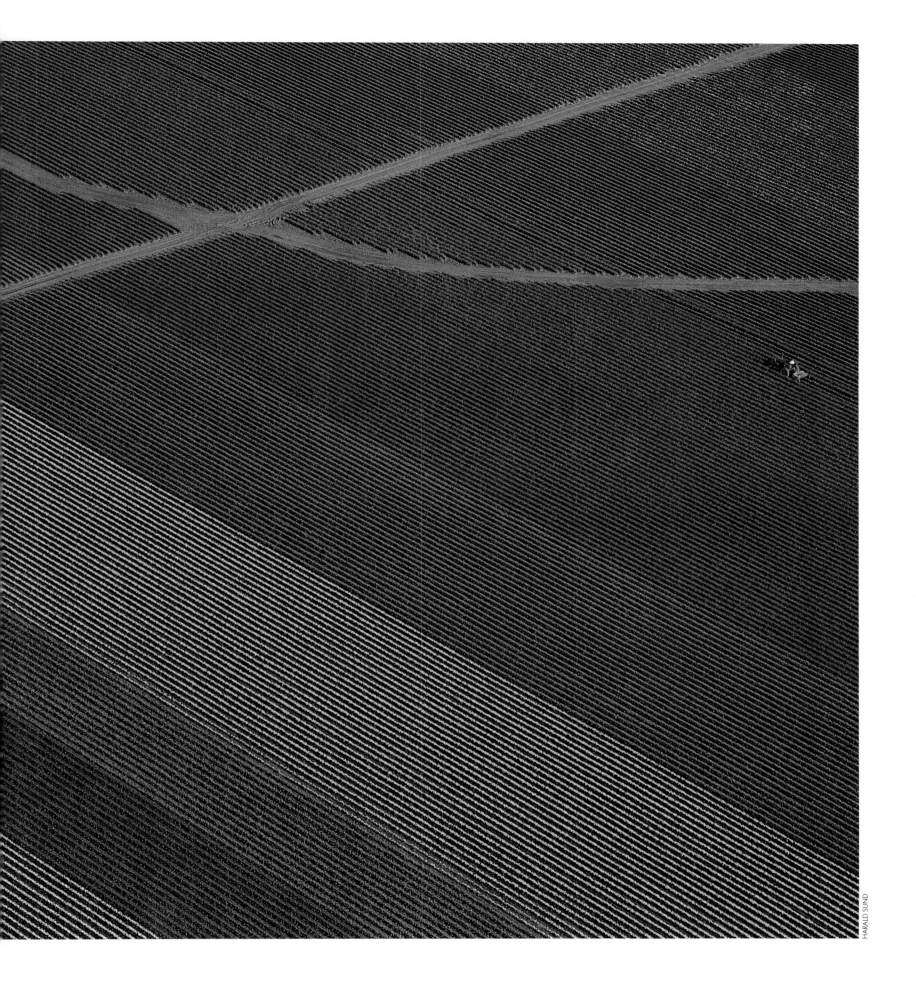

HARALD SUND

HARALD SUND

Western Washington University stands atop a hill looking down on Bellingham, a city with many fastidiously preserved Victorian mansions built in the glorious days of sawmilling. The city was formed in 1903 with the merger of three rival towns—Fairhaven, New Whatcom and Sehome. At various stages its economy has featured fishing, coal mining, and shipbuilding. It has just become the new Washington terminal for the Alaska Ferry System.

Sandy Point, lined with vacation and year-round homes built on land leased from the Lummi Indians, separates the shallow waters of Bellingham Bay from Hale Passage. Lummi Island, a nesting place for potters and artists, looms in the background.

HARALD SUND

*I*n the early days of Washington logging, the felled trees were dragged by oxen to the water over skidroads of logs and then floated to the mill. Later, logging railroads were pushed into the forest. Now trucks, such as these gathered for a loggers' festival at Deming, are the prime movers. High climbing, log sawing, birling, and a truck rodeo are features of such exhibitions.

153

HARALD SUND

When surveyors determined the exact location of the 49th parallel marking the United States-Canadian boundary they found that it cut across the tip of a peninsula extending from British Columbia into Birch Bay. Two and a half square miles of the mainland became in effect an American island attached to the mainland. Suggestions that the area, Point Roberts, be internationalized have gained little support.

Sam Hill, a wealthy promoter of good highways and good international relations, paid, in 1921, for the construction of the Peace Arch at Blaine where Interstate 5 reaches the border, The Arch celebrates the undefended border between "children of a common mother."

CHILDREN OF A COMMON MOTHER

EASTERN WASHINGTON

HARALD SUND

*E*arly settlers, misled by high yields from first plantings, built houses that could not be paid for when rains failed or the market tightened. A discouraged farmer's wife wrote her cousin, "We are beyond. We tell time by the sun and measure the months in baths."

EASTERN WASHINGTON

"Late in June the vast northwestern desert of wheat began to take on a tinge of gold, lending an austere beauty to that endless, rolling smooth world of treeless hills . . . A thousand hills lay bare to the sky, and half of every hill was wheat and half was fallow ground; and all of them, with the shallow valleys between, seemed big and strange and isolated . . . A lonely, hard, heroic country."

Zane Gray (*The Desert of Wheat*) 1919

Previous pages

The tawny hills of the Palouse, heavy with wheat.

GEORG GERSTER

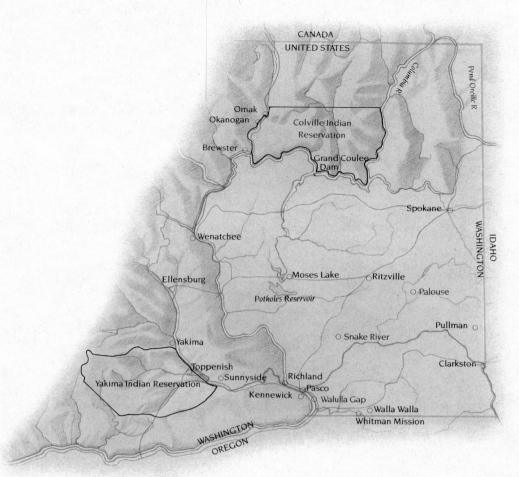

E ast of the Cascades, or as Washingtonians put it, "on the dry side of the mountains," the air is clear, trees stand separately, there is a sense of space. On the wet side, one is always conscious of lush growth and the nearness of the ocean. Across the mountains, one is in the presence of naked geology, aware of the primordial forces that shaped the vast landscape.

Three hundred million years ago, geologists say, the waves of the Pacific broke on the coast of Idaho. The area that was to become Washington lay beneath the surface, a submerged shelf accumulating sediment from the run-off of the continent; sediment slowly turning into rock. Then, according to a scenario based on the estimated paths of tectonic plates, a portion of the earth's crust wrenched loose from the spreading rift in the Pacific floor and bumped into the western edge of the continental plate, compressing the sedimentary rock and folding it into ridges that broke through the ocean surface. Eroded fragments can still be seen in the northeastern corner of the State.

Fifty million years later a drifting plate deposited the granitic North Cascades, tilted, fractured and laced with scrapings of sediment. Pressure from another roaming plate sliding under the lip of the continent caused coastal lands to rise and buckle, forming mountain ranges.

Between 12 and 15 million years ago, thin, superheated magma began welling from vents in the interior of Washington; rock so hot it could flow a hundred miles or more before cooling to a halt. In central Washington, where the magma was deepest, it formed a vast plate of basalt. The weight of 90 cubic miles of basalt spread across central Washington caused the earth's crust to sag in the middle of the pool and to tilt upward toward the edges. The ancestral Columbia River, diverted forcibly from its old course, swung west to skirt the mass. Thus began the Columbia Basin.

Time ticked off in the million-year units of geology. Within the past 700,000 years, volcanoes—Baker, Glacier, Rainier, Adams, St. Helens and Hood—sprouted and bloomed along the western side of the Cascade range. Behind the range, there was little rain. The mountains forced the wet air from the Pacific to rise, cooling it, squeezing out the moisture and creating an arid zone that stretched eastward for a thousand miles. But wind and glaciers worked on the deep carpet of basalt, turning the surface to soil.

Toward the end of the last ice age, only 15,000 years ago, a finger from the continental ice field poked down from British Columbia in the trough now occupied by the Pend Oreille Lake, then pushed eastward up the Clark Fork valley. It blocked drainage from the east with an ice wall 2,500 feet high. A lake formed behind the ice dam. It grew to cover 3,000 square miles and to hold 500 cubic miles of water.

The cataclysm that followed could have been seen from the moon. The ice dam burst. A wall of water, hundreds of feet high, pushing winds of hurricane force ahead of it, surged across northern Idaho and eastern Washington, piled against the Cascades in a temporary lake covering thousands of square miles, then funnelled through the Walulla Gap—the route carved through the Cascades by the Columbia River. The flow of water was sixty times that of the Amazon and ten times that of all the rivers in the world today.

Geologists think there may have been a series of ice dams and floods, the last occurring about 13,000 years ago, after the arrival of the first humans in the land. Since the ice age, soils have formed, forests have grown, died and been reborn, rivers have changed course. But, except for the vanished top of Mount St. Helens, the landscape is little changed in the geological sense. Water, wind and winter cold continue to erode the deposits, turning the basalt of the Columbia Basin into the rich, arid soil of what came to be called the Great Columbia Plain.

Early visitors wrote it off as desert. The first whites to report its existence were Lewis and Clark. President Jefferson in 1804 dispatched the Corps of Discovery on what he optimistically described as "a Passage through the Garden." They were to determine if there was "a direct and practicable water communication across this continent for the purpose of commerce." There was none. And as garden, most of the route they followed lay through land badly in need of watering.

Their first glimpse of Washington, from across the Snake River which they had reached from the Clearwater, revealed the low plain on which the town of Clarkston now stands. Clark found it "worthey of remark" that there was "no one stick of timber on the river near the forks." And as they bumped down the Snake in their crude dugouts, the hills grew steeper, deeply rutted, exposing the "dark ruged Stone" of the basaltic platform on which the plain rests. Little vegetation was noted other than "a bearded grass about three inches high" and three species of prickly pear. Wood was so scarce that Lewis and Clark broke their own rule and used house boards, which Indians had stored on the river bank, for fuel.

Nowhere on their downstream passage through the Columbia Plain did the explorers see land they thought of as agricultural. What impressed them as a resource was salmon, so abundant that Indians sometimes used dried salmon for fuel. Not until their homeward journey in 1805, when the friendly Walla Walla Indians suggested a shortcut to the Clearwater that led them to an area of richer, dark soil and "a plenty of wood, water and game," did they find land they could praise. Even then they noted that although it resembled the plains of Missouri, it was "not enlivened by the vast herds of buffaloe Elk &c. which ornament the other."

The Lewis and Clark expedition ended the search for a transcontinental waterway, but brought the Americans into rivalry with the British in the quest for a land route. John Jacob Astor in 1810 sent expeditions by land and sea to establish a post at the mouth of the Columbia River. The sea party arrived first, on March 22, 1811; groups from the overland party, which had had a terrible crossing, straggled in over the next few months.

The British were already present in the Pacific Northwest, though not at the mouth of the Columbia. Alexander Mackenzie, exploring on behalf of the North West Company, had found a route through the Canadian Rockies to the sea, north of Vancouver Island, in 1793. Another North West Company fur trader and explorer, David Thompson, crossed the Rockies with his Indian wife and children in 1807. He built the first company trading post, Kootenay House, just north of Lake Windermere and began unravelling the peculiarly complicated courses of the upper Columbia River and its tributaries.

In 1810 Thompson's men established a trading post, Spokane House, a few miles from the falls on the river that gave what is now Spokane its name. The following year, having worked out the pattern of rivers in northeastern Washington and the Idaho panhandle, Thompson fulfilled his dream of descending the Columbia to its mouth. At a camp beside the little Blaebury he noted in his journal on June 2 that the "current descends to the Pacific ocean—may God in his mercy give me to see where its water flows into the ocean, and return in safety."

A month later, having reached Kettle Falls on the Columbia, Thompson and his small party built a canoe sheathed with shiplapped cedar strips rather than the traditional birch bark. On July 3, 1811, they set off on what Thompson called "the journey of the summer moon." Indians of different tribes danced prayers for the strangers' safe passage as they reached the tributary streams—the seeping Sanpoil, the fertile-terraced Okanogan, the cascading Chelan, the canyon-girt Wenatchee, and the sage-surrounded Yakima—all carrying snowmelt from the eastern slopes of the Cascades and its guardian volcanoes on the western horizon. Thompson paused to thank the dancers with gifts of tobacco and promises of trading posts to be established.

On the sandy point where the Columbia joins the Snake, where Lewis and Clark had spent a day checking the latitude, Thompson tarried only long enough to drive in a stake to which he fastened a proclamation claiming the area for king, country and company: "Know hereby that this country is claimed by Great Britain as part of its territories, and the N.W. Company of Merchants from Canada, finding the factory for this place [Spokane House] inconvenient for them, do hereby intend to erect a factory in this place for the commerce of the country around. Thompson. July 9, 1811."

Downstream again, through "rapids most fierce," they skirted disaster until suddenly the Cascades folded back like wings—Mount Hood on the left, St. Helens on the right—and only the wind-raised waves of the tidal estuary between them and their goal. On July 15, following the southern bank of a river widened into a bay and tasting of salt, they saw in a niche on the forested shore a cluster of log buildings—the three-month-old outpost that Americans styled Fort Astoria.

For Thompson, the presence of rivals was a disappointment. From the beginning, the North West Company had been battling a rival far more formidable than Astor—the licensed monopoly of the Hudson's Bay Company. And many of the Astorians were old friends, Canadians who had gained their familiarity with the fur trade

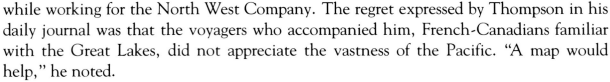

while working for the North West Company. The regret expressed by Thompson in his daily journal was that the voyagers who accompanied him, French-Canadians familiar with the Great Lakes, did not appreciate the vastness of the Pacific. "A map would help," he noted.

A map! Since Thompson's arrival in the United States at the age of 14 years, apprenticed to the Hudson's Bay Company from a charity school, he had been drawn to cartography. He had left the Hudson's Bay Company for the North West Company because it promised more opportunity for map-making. Now he could boast in the privacy of his journal: "Thus I have fully completed the survey of this part of North America from sea to sea and by almost innumerable astronomical observations have determined the positions of the mountains, lakes and rivers and other remarkable places to the northern part of this continent . . . the work of 27 years."

When Thompson started back up the Columbia, after eight days of socializing, it was alongside a party led by Robert Stuart, a 26-year-old Scot who had been hired away from the North West Company by Astor. They kept company as far as the Okanogan, where the Stuart group knocked together a shack—Fort Okanogan—which they left in the care of young Ross Alexander and his dog Weasel.

Thompson went back across the Rockies and recorded his findings on his monumental map of northern America. This map helped to guide British fur traders along a river route that enabled an express canoe to carry a message from the St. Lawrence to the Pacific in one hundred days (most trips took longer).

Meanwhile Robert Stuart was sent back from Astoria to St. Louis. His trip took 10 months. Along the line, men of the Stuart party were reduced to drinking their own urine to prevent dehydration. They celebrated the New Year in 1813 by smoking a tobacco pouch. And they crossed the Rockies through the unpublicized South Pass, a feat they soon made known. South Pass proved to be low enough, wide enough and sufficiently snow free to permit passage of wagons. It was the key to the Oregon Trail.

British domination of the seas during the War of 1812 forced the Astorians to sell out to the North West Company. The Hudson's Bay Company later absorbed the North West Company's posts and dominated the fur trade in the entire Oregon country. But in 1836 two American missionary families, the Whitmans and the Spaldings, came through South Pass in a covered wagon. From then on, the contest for occupation was between single Britons paddling canoes and American families rolling west on wheels.

At the height of the border controversy, with American expansionists bellowing "Fifty-four Forty or Fight," meaning the United States should go to war if necessary to gain title to all the land north to the Russian-American boundary at 54° 40', a congressman assured the country that war was not necessary. "We will win Oregon in our bedrooms. We will outbreed them." By 1846, United States citizens outnumbered the subjects of the British Crown west of the Rockies; though few Americans were north of the Columbia, they were in a position to spill over.

The high falls of the Palouse. "The water falls in one perpendicular sheet of about 600 feet in height, from between rocks of greyish-yellow colour, which rise about 400 feet above the summit of the fall," as Paul Kane wrote in his *Journal* on July 14, 1847.

British Prime Minister Robert Peel, a man of peace in his last days of office and fearful of what his hawkish successor might do, agreed to a boundary settlement. The line would run from the crest of the Rockies along the 49th parallel to the middle of the Strait of Georgia, then south through the undefined "principal channel" threading through the San Juan archipelago and westward down the middle of the Strait of Juan de Fuca to the Pacific. The Americans won their desired harbors on Puget Sound. The British retained all of Vancouver Island.

War with the British had been avoided, but what about the Indians? The United States government had adopted the position that, until the various ill-defined Indian nations had ceded their lands in formal treaties ratified by the Senate and signed by the President, whites could not receive title to property. The situation in the Pacific Northwest was especially complicated. During the period of joint occupation by Great Britain and the United States thousands of immigrants had arrived, chosen land and proceeded with development. The Provisional Government of Oregon, which functioned before Oregon Territory was formed, granted settlers title to such land, but the Organic Act of 1848 passed by Congress to create the Territory annulled such grants and restored Indian rights until treaties were ratified.

When Congress split Oregon Territory, creating Washington, no treaties were in effect. Settlers were edgy, impatient to have property rights settled. Isaac Stevens, the 35-year-old West Pointer rewarded with the Territorial Governorship for political services to President Franklin Pierce, was impatient by nature.

In 1854-55 he embarked on a whirlwind campaign to get the Indians to agree to sell most of their land to the United States and retire to reservations. In three months of negotiations with western Washington tribes he managed to get agreement on four treaties. Then he summoned four powerful tribes in eastern Washington to meet with him on the council ground in Walla Walla. After days of tense negotiation, leaders of the Walla Walla, Cayuse, Yakima and Nez Perce were persuaded to sign a treaty ceding to the United States 47,000 square miles of the Inland Empire.

"Thus ended in the most satisfactory manner this great council," Stevens wrote in his journal before riding off to meet with tribes in Montana. But the Indians he left behind did not share his satisfaction. The more they thought about the treaty the less they liked it. While they waited for word from Washington D.C. that the "Council of Old Men" had approved the treaty, and the "Great White Father" had signed it and the promised payments were on their way, gold was discovered near Fort Colville.

There was not a great deal of gold, but a prospector with a pan could make $5–15 a day—this at a time when common labor paid $40 a month, and the pickings had grown thin in the California gold fields. A rush began. The shortest route from the south to the Colville area lay through the Yakima valley. There were incidents. Some prospectors were killed, and Indians said the prospectors had raped Indian women. The local Indian agent went to investigate and disappeared. Troops sent to punish the Yakima were driven back across the Columbia. It was war.

Hostilities spread to western Washington when a civilian militia attempted to take Leschi, a Nisqually who wanted the treaty revised, into protective custody. Some warriors followed Leschi into the hills. Fighting was sporadic in the Puget Sound area

*E*llensburg, astride the Yakima River on the eastern slope of the Cascades, celebrates its diverse ranching, farming, and lumber economy with a three-day rodeo that ends on Labor Day each year.

where the white population was concentrated. The war settled into a siege within a siege—the Indian guerrillas keeping the whites off their farms, penned in behind stockades, while white militia forces kept the hostile Indians away from their customary fishing and gathering areas and rounded up the "friendlies" on reservations. After 11 months, and one markedly unsuccessful Indian attack on Seattle, the war in the west was over.

East of the mountains the Indians were numerous, more united and, with their horses, more mobile than their coastal counterparts. The civilian volunteers who came to subdue them were poorly trained, badly armed and indifferently led by their elected officers who, in most cases, were unfamiliar with the terrain. The only thing they had too much of was confidence. They seldom caught up with the foe except when the Indians, in ambush, wanted them to.

When at last federal reinforcements appeared, the army officers and Governor Stevens could agree on neither strategy nor tactics. Stevens carried on an independent campaign with short-term volunteers. He financed the war with scrip issued against the federal treasury, running up a debt of a million dollars, which Congress for several years refused to pay. In the course of the war Stevens declared martial law, arrested and jailed the Chief Justice of the Territorial Supreme Court, an excess for which he was eventually reprimanded and fined.

Not until the fall of 1858, three years after the outbreak of hostilities, did the regular army maneuver the main force of the enemy into position for a showdown in the hills overlooking Four Lakes near Spokane. Before battle was joined, the army was able to capture most of the Indian horses, some 800 of them, depriving the enemy of both mobility and emergency rations. The Indians surrendered unconditionally. Their horses were killed, and some of the war leaders hanged. The tribes moved onto reservations.

The Inland Empire was open for exploitation. More prospectors travelled to the Colville region, then to strikes in the Jefferson Basin (in what was then Washington Territory but became western Montana) and to the diggings between the Coeur d'Alene and Salmon Rivers (in what, after 1863, was Idaho). Other prospectors moved up the valleys of the Okanogan and Kettle on their way to the Fraser River and Cariboo rushes.

Miners had to be supplied. Small towns grew up to meet their needs, each boasting at least one bar that claimed to be "one of the longest bars north of San Francisco and east of Portland." Cattle—"provender provided with hooves"—were driven in from Oregon. The bitter winter of 1860 destroyed most of the animals already on the Columbia Plain, and the price of beef rose dramatically. Ben Snipes gambled on buying more than a thousand head in the Willamette Valley at prices ranging from $6 to $16 a head, and driving them to the Cariboo where, he had been told, the half-dollar was the smallest coin used and three fried eggs cost $2. He sold his critters for an average of $100 apiece and rode nervously back to the State with $100,000 in gold dust in his saddlebags and a new reputation as the "Cattle King of Oregon." Snipes's success brought more cattle into eastern Washington than could be sold. The herds multiplied in the bunch grass country of the Columbia Basin, and there were annual drives through the Cascade passes to the markets of Puget Sound.

At the height of the gold excitement, miners would pay a dollar a pound for flour. Settlers who stayed on the farm planted wheat, which did well in the valleys. By 1867 there was a surplus in the Walla Walla area, and a banker named Dorsey Baker became a hero and a legend by building the Walla Walla to Wallula railroad to carry the grain to the Columbia for transport downstream to Portland on the vessels of the Oregon Steam Navigation Company, whose rates were also a legend. Baker's line entered folklore as the "Rawhide Railroad" because, it was said, strips of strap iron were tied on top of the wooden rails with leather thongs.

Another legendary entrepreneur was H. F. Smith, a gold hunter who in 1860 stopped roaming and built a cabin on the eastern shore of Lake Osoyoos in the Okanogan valley. As the valley's first settler he became its first representative to the territorial legislature in Olympia. To get to the 1865 session, Smith had to go north into British Columbia, cross the mountains to Fort Langley, then proceed by passenger boat down the Fraser River, Georgia Strait and Puget Sound to reach Olympia. At Hope, on his return trip, he bought 1,200 seedling apple trees and some peach trees, which he carried by snowshoe and dog sled across the mountains to his homestead. The orchard he established on the sunny river bank prospered. Some of his trees are still bearing fruit, and today there are nearly two million apple trees in the Okanogan valley.

The legends of Smith, Baker and Snipes—the Apple Baron, the Cattle King and the Rawhide Railroad Builder—have a common theme. They all prospered by finding solutions to the basic problems posed by Washington's topography—the difficulty of getting through the Cascade Range.

Alfalfa is harvested from the rich soil near Richland.

Following pages

Ever since sod was broken to raise food
for prospectors, wheat has been the dominant
crop on the rolling hills of Walla Walla county.

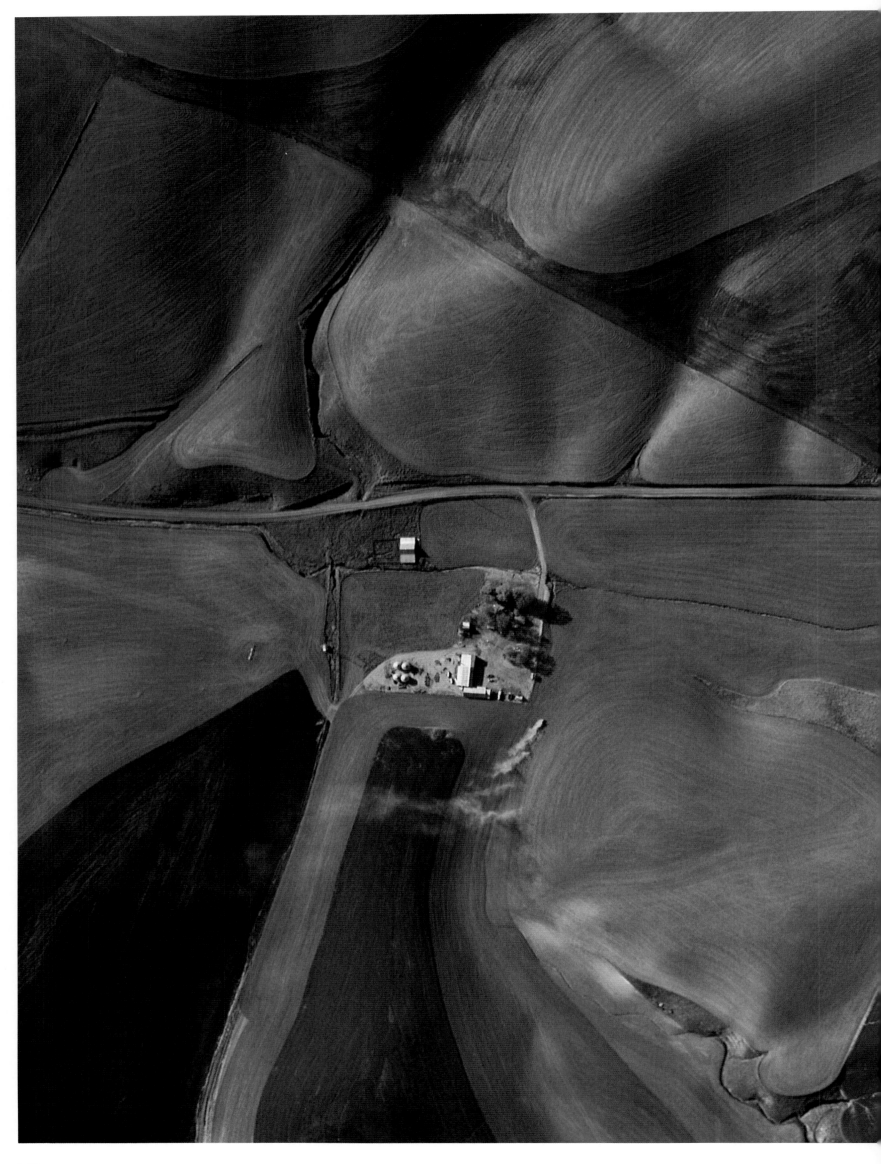

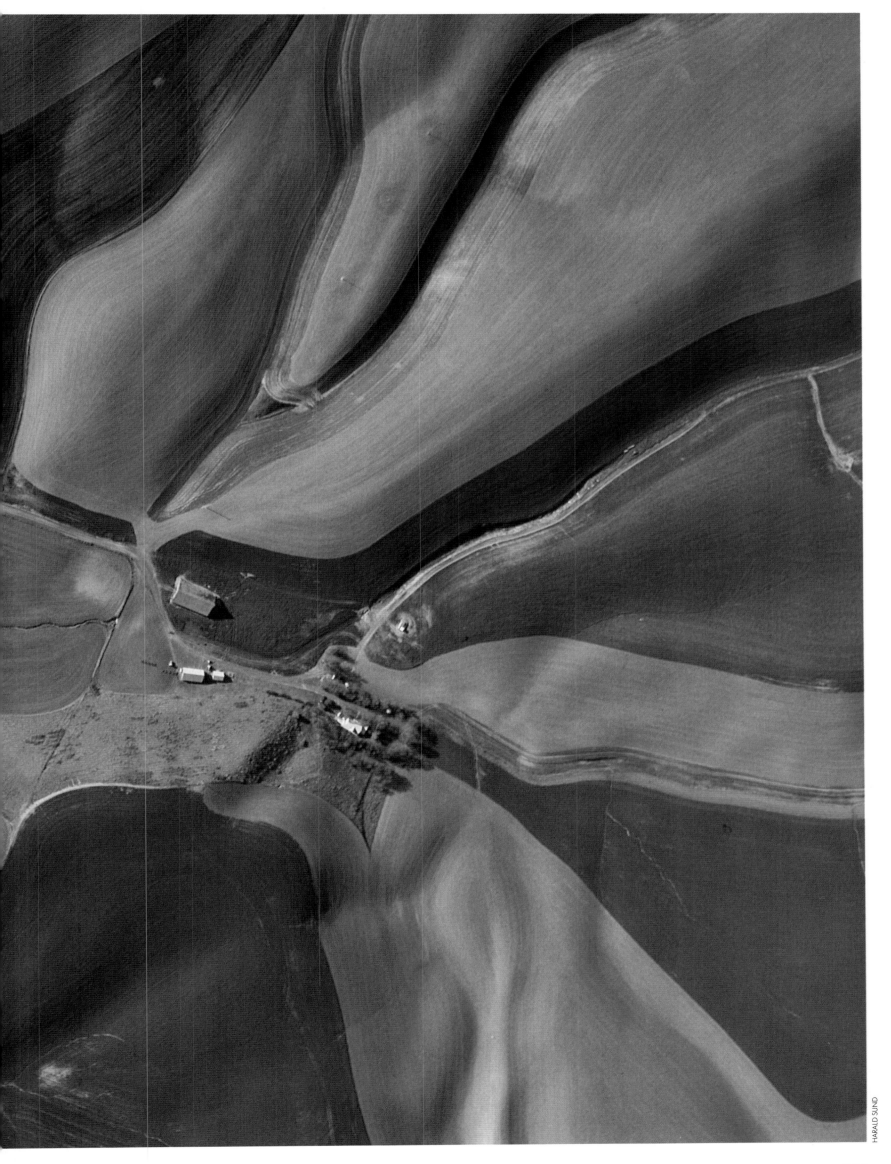

HARALD SUND

Left

Near this ranchland in Colfax county, Lieutenant Colonel Edward J. Steptoe's troops were defeated by the Spokane Indians in what proved to be the last Indian victory in the Treaty Wars of 1854-58. The green patches are pea vines still ripening.

Previous pages

"We were at it 13 hours a day, sometimes far out among the wheat-covered hills that were so steep they seemed to lean over from the top; again at the big threshing machine, whose howling cylinder and rumbling wilderness of mechanism seemed to be yelling 'Wheat, wheat, wheat, more wheat!' all the time," wrote Joe Ashlock, in *Washington Farmer,* in July 1919.

Farming the rich black soil along the Walla Walla River was begun near here, on a 300-acre site chosen in October 1836, by Marcus Whitman for use by the American Board of Commissioners for Foreign Missions. The following March, using two oxen borrowed from a Cayuse chief, a bull owned by the missionary board and another loaned by the Hudson's Bay Company, two horses and four mules, Whitman was able to turn a few acres of sod and plant peas, corn, and potatoes.

173

174

Strip farming is much practiced in the Palouse. Bands of fallow soil lie between the contoured strips of ripening grain. Light in color and light in weight, the Palouse loess is carried in by wind and water. It darkens at the surface as organic matter decays.

Following pages

Some 20,000 spectators gathered on the campus of Walla Walla high school in May 1988 to watch the ascent of 50 balloons at the fourteenth annual Hot Air Balloon Stampede.
HARALD SUND

Pages 178-179

The Whitman Mission at Waiilatpu, "the place of rye grass," was destroyed by the Cayuse in November 1847. Marcus and Narcissa Whitman, and 11 others were killed. Their efforts had not resulted in a single conversion to Christianity. The tragedy virtually ended the Protestant missionary effort among the Indians of the Pacific Northwest.

Spokane, second largest city in Washington and the largest inland metropolis west of Omaha and north of Denver, straddles the Spokane River on terraces beside its major falls. Spokane is the unofficial capital of the Inland Empire, an ill-defined expanse bounded only by heavy rainfall. Settlement in the immediate vicinity of Spokane did not begin until cattlemen from Montana took claims in 1871. While establishing itself as the economic nexus of an extensive area, Spokane has managed to maintain the ambience of a city small enough for neighborly enjoyment.

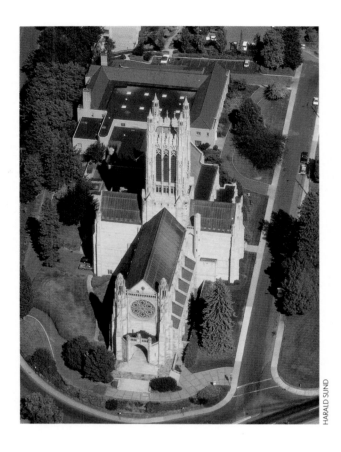

St. John's Episcopal Cathedral, to the design of architect Harold Whitehouse, exemplifies the English Gothic revival style and the free flow of material. The sandstone is from Wilkeson, the limestone from Indiana.

Established in 1887 by Father Joseph Cataldo as a Jesuit school for boys, Gonzaga became a college in 1894 and was elevated to university status in 1922. Its well-organized archives contain a rare deposit of information from the Jesuit missions in the Pacific Northwest and Alaska.

*E*xpo '74, Spokane's 1974 world fair, turned the neglected banks of the city's namesake river into a community playground. The crowd assembled below Burlington Northern Tower is celebrating Credit Union Day.

GEORG GERSTER

*T*he remarkable development of eastern Washington agriculture rests largely on research done at Washington State University in Pullman, which, when established in 1891, bore the name "Washington State Agricultural College, Experiment Station, and School of Science." WSU's experimental farms have developed a succession of strains of wheat ideally suited to the terrain, soil conditions, and climate of the region. They have fulfilled H. L. Davis's prediction in the prize-winning novel *Honey in the Horn:* "The land, by some mysterious impulse . . . was going to raise ton lots of everything—cattle, hogs, sheep, chickens, turkeys, geese, silver foxes, strawberries, gooseberries, apples, peaches, plums, garden truck, flax, cut flowers. The climate would cure asthma, tuberculosis, rickets, melancholia, goiter. It was going to be a remarkable region."

HARALD SUND

*B*efore crops, there were critters or cattle. And after crops there are cattle still, but not so many. Here at the Tri-Cities some await shipment as fresh meat. This is not a cow wash. The water is being sprayed to keep down dust.

HARALD SUND

Many academic agronomists discourage the burning of stubble after wheat harvest on the theory that plowing under organic matter helps the soil. Many farmers continue to burn on the theory that it discourages disease. This field is near Moses Lake.

HARALD SUND

Sometimes the railroad is not enough. Even on rich land with irrigation, things go wrong. The market is poor, the bank cannot wait, the family gives up. An abandoned farm, near Sprague.

The pattern of success: combines are parked by the farmhouse and work buildings on a handsome spread near Ritzville. Phil Ritz took a claim here in 1878. A group of German-Russians arrived soon after. Their hard work paid off when the Northern Pacific came through the area, opening up a market for their produce.

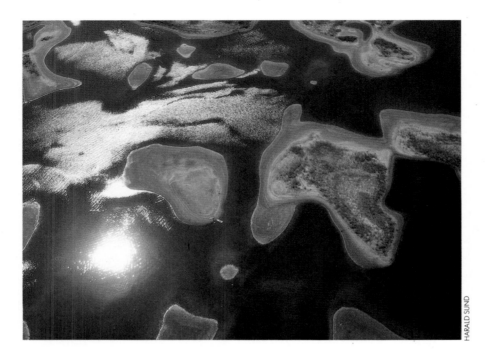

HARALD SUND

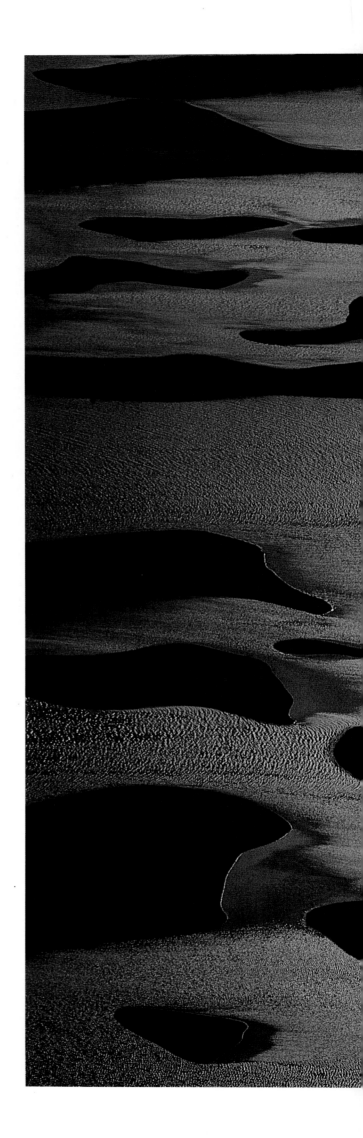

As the ice age glaciers melted, sand was carried southward and eastward by the floods and spread across the basalt base of the plateau. The prevailing southerly winds have scooped out the sand and piled up dunes on the leeward side. Water held in the potholes provides a "pit stop" for wildfowl on their southward fall migrations.

Following pages

Pockets of fertile soil lie in the jumble of basalt islands and mesa-like humps of the channeled scablands. Wheat ranchers plant to within inches of the rock.

191

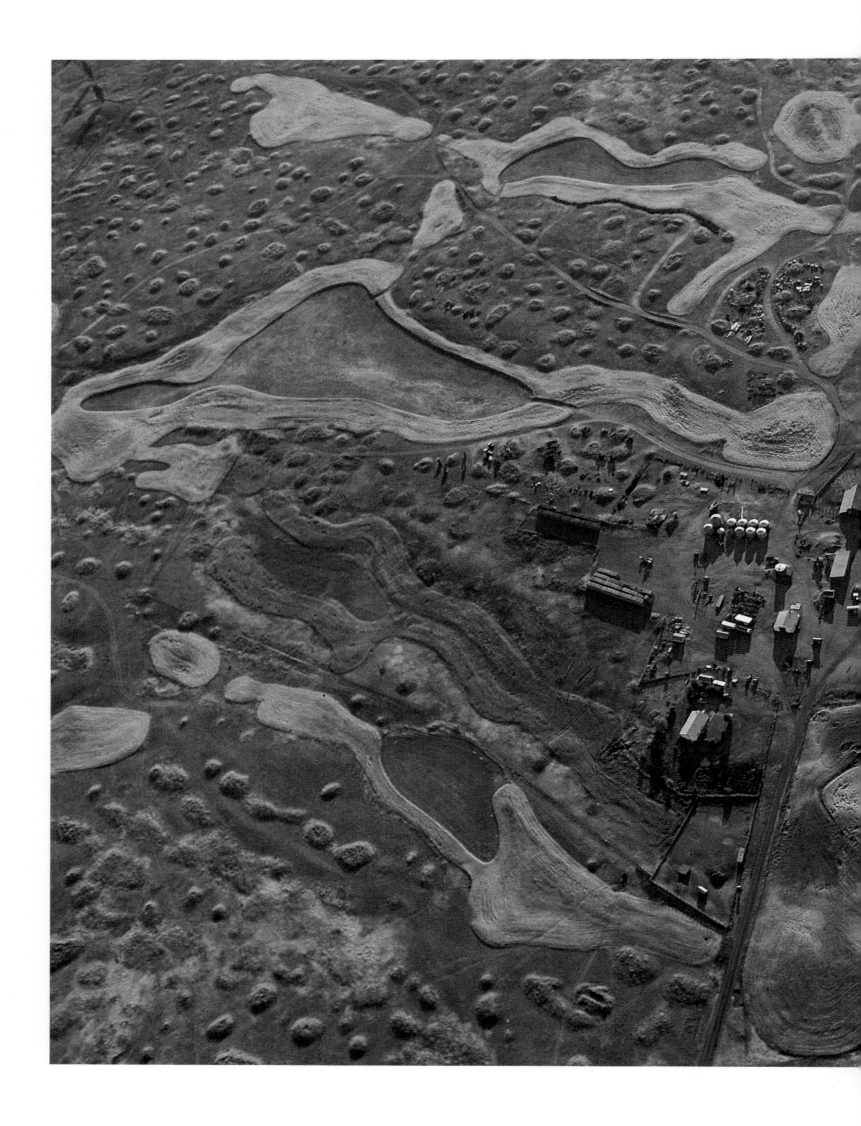

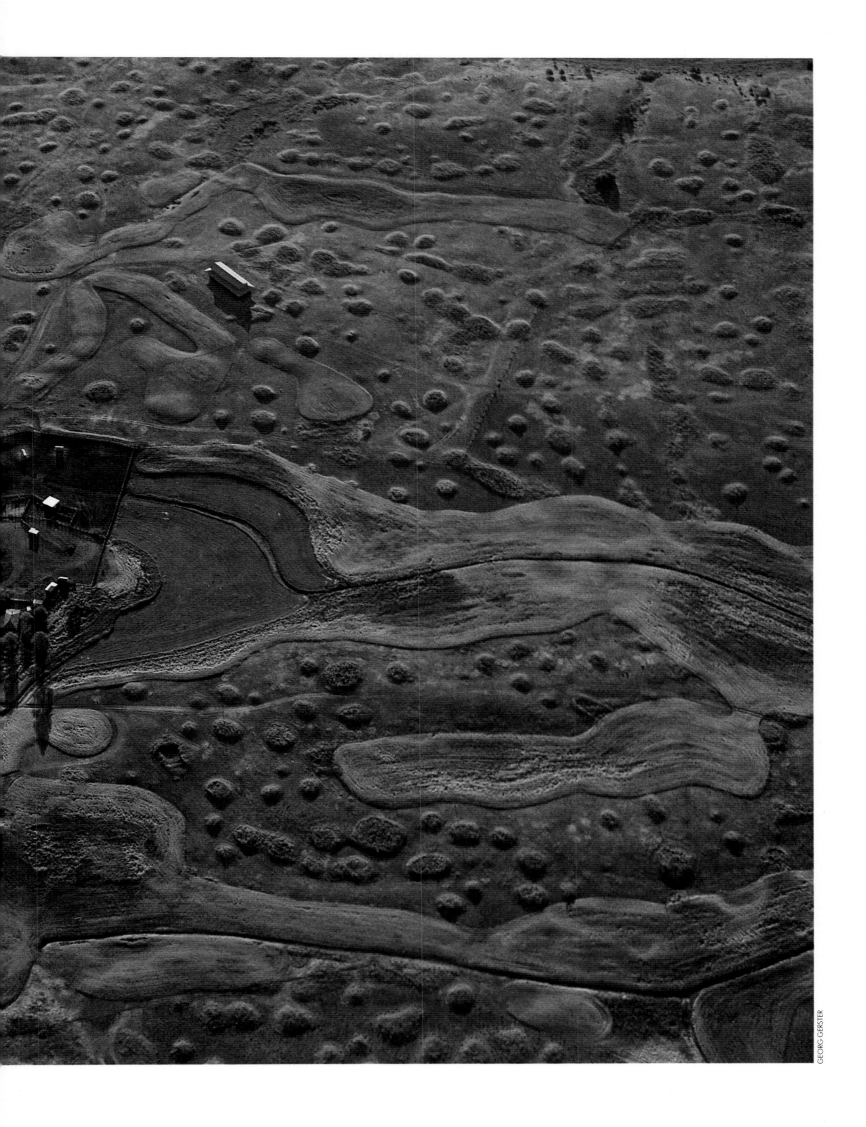

193

GEORG GERSTER

*V*ast honeycombs of apple boxes are stacked beside a Wenatchee orchard awaiting the harvest. Migrant labor comes from as far away as Central America to help with picking and sorting the apples for export.

*I*rrigation has turned the Yakima valley and the Columbia benchlands around Wenatchee into a vast orchard. Washington produces a third of the nation's apples – mostly Red Delicious and Yellow Delicious – as well as many other fruits.

*I*ndians of the Inland Empire were horsemen, accustomed to covering wide areas in seasonal trips to hunting grounds and fishing sites. The tradition continues with annual intertribal gatherings such as the Omak Stampede in the valley of the Okanogan.

HARALD SUND

HARALD SUND

*I*n Hudson's Bay Company days the junction of the Okanogan and the Columbia rivers was a place to leave messages for the next fur brigade passing by. Today a COMSAT station outside Brewster provides instant satellite communication with the outside world.

HARALD SUND

*F*ields of corn, wheat, and potatoes pattern the Horse Heaven Hills. To the west, Mount Hood, Mount Adams and Mount Rainier crown the Cascades. Topless Mount St. Helens has bowed out of the scene. *Right:* The vast reservoirs of the federal Columbia Basin Irrigation Project have led to improvements in irrigation technology. Most recent is the center-pivot system in which a radial arm, up to a quarter of a mile long, rotates in a great circle, propelled by the water it ejects.

HARALD SUND

*T*he area around Goldendale, the scene of early triumphs by the Yakima Indians over regular army forces in the early days of the Treaty Wars, is now devoted to small farms such as this one marked by a barn of exceptional redness.

*F*ields of rape, grown for seed that has a 30-45 per cent oil content, form on a forested hill a pattern that resembles a collage by Hans Arp.

HARALD SUND

A combine harvester and its carrier trace patterns in a field of wheat in the Pasco-Kennewick area.

A circle sprinkler fed by water from the federal irrigation system paints an abstract in alfalfa on the once arid plain near the Hanford Reservation.

HARALD SUND

Crescent Bar is a recently developed recreational and retirement community downstream from Wenatchee on the Columbia. Wind-surfing rivals golf as the favorite sport.

Following pages

Most early travellers followed the Columbia downstream but some followed the smaller rivers upstream into the mountains. The Longmire party found a path for covered wagons, the Northern Pacific for rails. The Yakima River and its valley invite an approach to Mount Rainier from the east.

HARALD SUND

For more than a century Pasco has been the nexus of rail communication. Here, near the juncture of the Snake and Columbia rivers, transcontinental rail lines converge. To reach western Washington they must either follow the Columbia downstream or climb through one of the mountain passes to Puget Sound. The Tri-City freight yards are the most active in Washington.

THE CASCADES

HARALD SUND

"The Far Northwest is a vast wilderness
waiting like a rich heiress to be
appropriated and enjoyed," Samuel
Wilkeson wrote Jay Cooke in 1870.

THE CASCADES

Mountains interposed
Make enemies of nations, who had else
Like kindred drops been mingled into one.

William Cowper

Previous pages

Barrier and playground, the Cascades
divide Washington from Canada through
to Oregon.

HARALD SUND

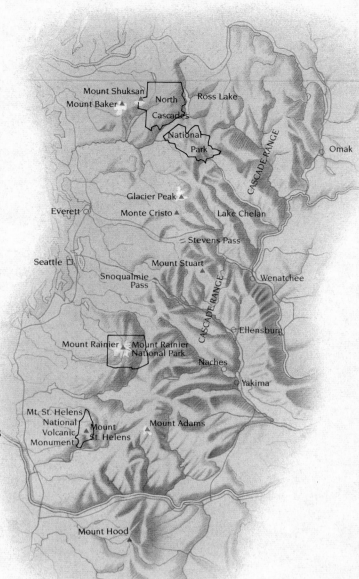

The Cascades seem ever present in Washington. From the west they are the horizon— sometimes a brooding green-black shrouded with mist, sometimes white crested and patterned with the extraordinary geometry of clearcut logging—but even in the dark, a presence. From the east they look more gentle—tawny in summer, the forest a tracery; in winter's clear air breathtakingly near and white. From either side, a boundary.

For several decades after Lewis and Clark, immigrants arriving in the Inland Empire by the Oregon Trail, even those intent on reaching Puget Sound, looked at the Cascades and decided the explorers had been well advised to follow nature's route, the Columbia, through the mountains.

Not that there were not established trails through the mountains. Indians had been crossing for trade, war and courtship for generations. The Nisquallies, first of the coastal Indians to become equestrian, trailed their purchases and stolen goods through Naches Pass. The Klickitats, who controlled the approaches to the pass and like robber-barons in Europe exacted tolls, may have given their name to, or received it from, the Salish tongue where *klickitat* is sometimes translated as robber.

Whites, too, had been through the pass. The Hudson's Bay Company sent supplies to the interior by pack trail. Pierre Charles, a Hudson's Bay Company employee, guided a party of Americans from the Wilkes expedition through Naches Pass on horseback in 1841. (The journey led the naturalist W. B. Brackenridge to observe that "a Sailor ashore is as a Fish out of Water," and also, "not two acres out of a hundred in the interior would repay a farmer's efforts.")

In 1853 concepts of the difficulty began to change. A Yakima Indian guided a Yankee tourist, Theodore Winthrop of the Massachusetts Winthrop family, through Naches on horseback. In his book *The Canoe and the Saddle* (published only after the young American became the first Yankee killed in the Civil War) Winthrop described the pass as perilous but enthralling. On the dry side he fell in with a survey party under brevet Captain George McClellan. The troops were lackadaisically carrying out an assignment to survey the Cascade passes for use as a military road or a railroad. McClellan found all unsuitable, including three later crossed by rail and five by highway.

The young officer's opinion may have suited Secretary of War Jefferson Davis, a Mississippi plantation owner who wanted any transcontinental rail system to run well south of the Mason-Dixon line. McClellan's opinion, however, was not well received by Isaac Stevens, the territorial Governor to whom McClellan reported. Stevens favored a northern route from the crest of the Rockies (which was then the eastern edge of Washington) to Puget Sound, running through the territory he governed.

In dismissing McClellan's conclusions, Stevens noted that in the same season while the surveyors were intoning "impassable," the first settlers made it through Naches Pass in wagons drawn by oxen. Not that they had it easy. They had to ford the Naches River 52 times, lower the wagons on ropes for 300 yards down the intimidating slant of Summit Hill then follow a sketchily blazed trail through thickening forest down the western slope, fording the Greenwater River 16 times and the White River six. Nobody perished, and of 36 wagons that started through the mountains 34 arrived. Furthermore, a local settler sent out by Stevens to confirm McClellan's report that snow made Snoqualmie Pass impassable in winter returned to say that snow depths in December were measurable in inches not feet.

In his first address to the territorial legislature, Stevens prophesied early completion of four transcontinental railroads. He urged the pioneers to do their duty and ask Congress for federal help in creating a road system. This they did. But Stevens's optimism was as overblown as McClellan's pessimism. Federal funds were limited and the distance between Washington D.C. and Washington Territory great. Congress had granted $20,000 for McClellan's survey, some of which went toward improving the trail through Naches Pass. The settlers called it the Emigrant Road. In theory it connected Walla Walla with Puget Sound, but as a barrier breaker it proved a failure. Most travellers took the longer dog-legged route to western Washington—down the Columbia, up the Cowlitz and across the prairie to salt water. East side and west side, road development ended when foothills began rising up to mountain height.

As for the transcontinental railroad, Congress did not act. Governor Stevens in 1857 persuaded the legislature to charter a "Northern Pacific" with authority for the incorporators to raise $15 million. They failed to raised 15 cents. During the Civil War, and after approving construction of the Union Pacific–Central Pacific to San Francisco, Congress issued a charter for a line to connect the Mississippi with Puget Sound. Funds were finally raised to start construction in 1870, but the Northern Pacific went bankrupt three years later. Rail transport did not reach Washington until 1883, and even then the tracks followed the Columbia on the Oregon side to Portland. Puget Sound was reached by a spur running up from Kalama on the Columbia. Not until 1887 was the Cascade section completed, allowing the produce of the Inland Empire to reach Puget Sound ports without first passing through Portland.

Meanwhile the legislature and King County raised $4,000 to improve the wagon trail across Snoqualmie Pass. After the money ran out in 1867 the road remained

The northwest flank of Mount Baker, Washington's northernmost volcano, seen from the west in winter, bathed in alpenglow
and with a full moon rising.

impassable to the United States postal service's mail mule. Henry Yesler offered his mill, the first steam sawmill in the State, as first prize in a lottery to raise money for road building. Not enough tickets were sold to allow for a draw to be made. Yesler kept the mill and made a fortune when waterfront prices rose.

Ironically, the first cross-State roadway, completed in 1896, went through the mountains at their most difficult section—the North Cascades, the spectacular jumble left by the collision of drifting continents. From Bellingham Bay the road skirted the southwest flank of the range to Marblemount, a hamlet that survived by supplying the occasional prospector. The road then worked upward, clinging to the lichen-coated walls of the canyons through which the Skagit River plunged. Reaching the crest of the Cascades at Washington Pass, it wound down through the pines to Twisp, crossed the Okanogan valley and terminated at Republic, on the banks of the Sanpoil River. The route was more useful to cowboys trailing cattle to Bellingham than to teamsters. As the aphorism of the day put it, "that road could stall an empty wagon going downhill." It fell into disrepair, then disuse and, finally, abandonment.

On level ground, technology was creating new demands for roads. The bicycle craze of the 1890s led to demand by the cycling enthusiasts for surfaced paths, hard as they might be on hooves. Then came the horseless carriage. By 1906 there were 763 registered "gas buggies" at large in Washington; a decade later, more than 70,000. Their owners quickly tired of parading Main Street.

In 1909 a racing-model Ford won a race from New York to Seattle staged to publicize Seattle's Alaska-Yukon-Pacific Exposition. It crossed the continent in a breathtaking 22 days and 56 minutes, a full day ahead of the second-place finisher. But it was the runner-up, the Shamut, "a comfortable, roomy touring car weighing 4,000 pounds," that drew a prophetic editorial in the Seattle *Star*: "It meets the demands of the average auto buyer. A car that can carry himself and his family or his friends with him. A car that is comfortable and roomy. A car that can endure, that is reliable, and that can speed some too, if speed is wanted in a pinch."

The Shamut did not survive, but other roomy touring cars helped to transform the Cascades from impediment to playground. To the displeasure of many ministers, driving to the mountains for a Sunday picnic became a middle-class pastime.

The mountains had been admired from a distance ever since George Vancouver described the "various rugged and grotesque shapes [that] rear their heads above the lofty pine trees that appear to compose one uninterrupted forest between us and the snow range." Naturalists like David Douglas wrote of the delights of camping: "McKay made us some fine steaks, and roasted a shoulder of doe for Breakfast, with an infusion of *Mentha borealis* [Canada mint] sweetened with a small portion of sugar. The meal laid on the clean mossy foliage of *Gaultheria Shallon* [salal] in lieu of a plate and our tea in a large wooden dish hewn out of the solid, and supping it with spoons made from the horns of the mountain sheep . . ." Now city folk could approximate such pleasures on a day's outing. Just crank up the "Tin Lizzie" and head for the hills.

Shuksan ("steep and rocky") is one of the few Washington mountains to retain its Indian name. The complicated mass of the 9,127-foot peak is seen from the west under a full moon.

The railroads, too, promoted the mountains as a recreation area. Even before the transcontinental reached the coast, the Northern Pacific was puffing the scenic grandeur of the American Alps, which were touted as not only handsome but health promoting. Several sanatoria for those with weak chests were built at high altitudes.

The Northern Pacific soon recognized another advantage of emphasizing the attractions of altitude. In return for building the line to the Pacific Northwest, the railroad received from federal lands a 200-foot right of way from the Mississippi to Puget Sound, plus 10 sections each of a square mile for every mile of track it laid in each State and 20 sections for every mile laid in each territory. That amounted to nearly two million acres of land, some at altitudes difficult to log and impossible to farm. The national interest in preserving wilderness areas had scored its first triumph with the creation of Yosemite National Park in 1872. The Northern Pacific was happy to encourage the movement for a Rainier National Park—and to trade glaciers and gravel for forest land that could be marketed.

The desire to preserve part of the natural heritage grew. In 1906 Congress gave the President authority to establish national monuments. Theodore Roosevelt created Mount Olympus National Monument in 1909. Thirty years later the Olympic National Park was created. In the 1960s a North Cascades National Park was established, as well as the Lake Chelan National Recreation Area and the Ross Lake National Recreation Area. There are now more than nine million acres of national forest land in Washington, most of it in the Cascades.

A pristine blanket of snow covers
Mount Rainier's Sunrise Lodge.

Snoqualmie Pass, with its summit at 3,004 feet, became the route for wagons crossing to Seattle. It remains the prime railway route, and is a favorite ski area, even at night.

Following pages

The Indians called Mount Baker, Komo Kulshan ("steep white mountain"). From its summit one looks across the foothills to the San Juan archipelago and the mountains of Vancouver Island.

HARALD SUND

HARALD SUND

*R*oss Lake, on the western slope, is an artificial lake. It lies behind Seattle City Light's dam on the Skagit River. The reservoir reaches into Canada. A tour boat, seen in the foreground, carries visitors almost to the border.

*T*he 1,500-foot deep trough holding 55-mile long Lake Chelan was gouged by an ice age glacier. The lake formed behind a glacial moraine that has been replaced by a dam. Chelan translates as "deep water."

Following pages

*G*lacier Peak, the most rarely visited of Washington's volcanos, rises in a roadless area directly east of Everett. Admired by wilderness hikers for its isolation, Glacier is renowned among geologists for an eruption 12,000 years ago that spread pumiceous ash as far as southern Alberta.

HARALD SUND

*I*n July 1889, a well-read but overly
optimistic prospector detected gleams of
ore on an escarpment of this peak. "It is
as rich as the Count of Monte Cristo,"
he exclaimed, thereby naming the
mountain. His strike proved to be as
fictitious as Alexander Dumas's count.

*M*ount Stuart, in the wilderness area of
the Wenatchee Mountains, was the
center of a temporary gold fever in the
1860s. Placer deposits were found in the
Swauk district nearby but, unlike this
sunset, now gleam only in memory.

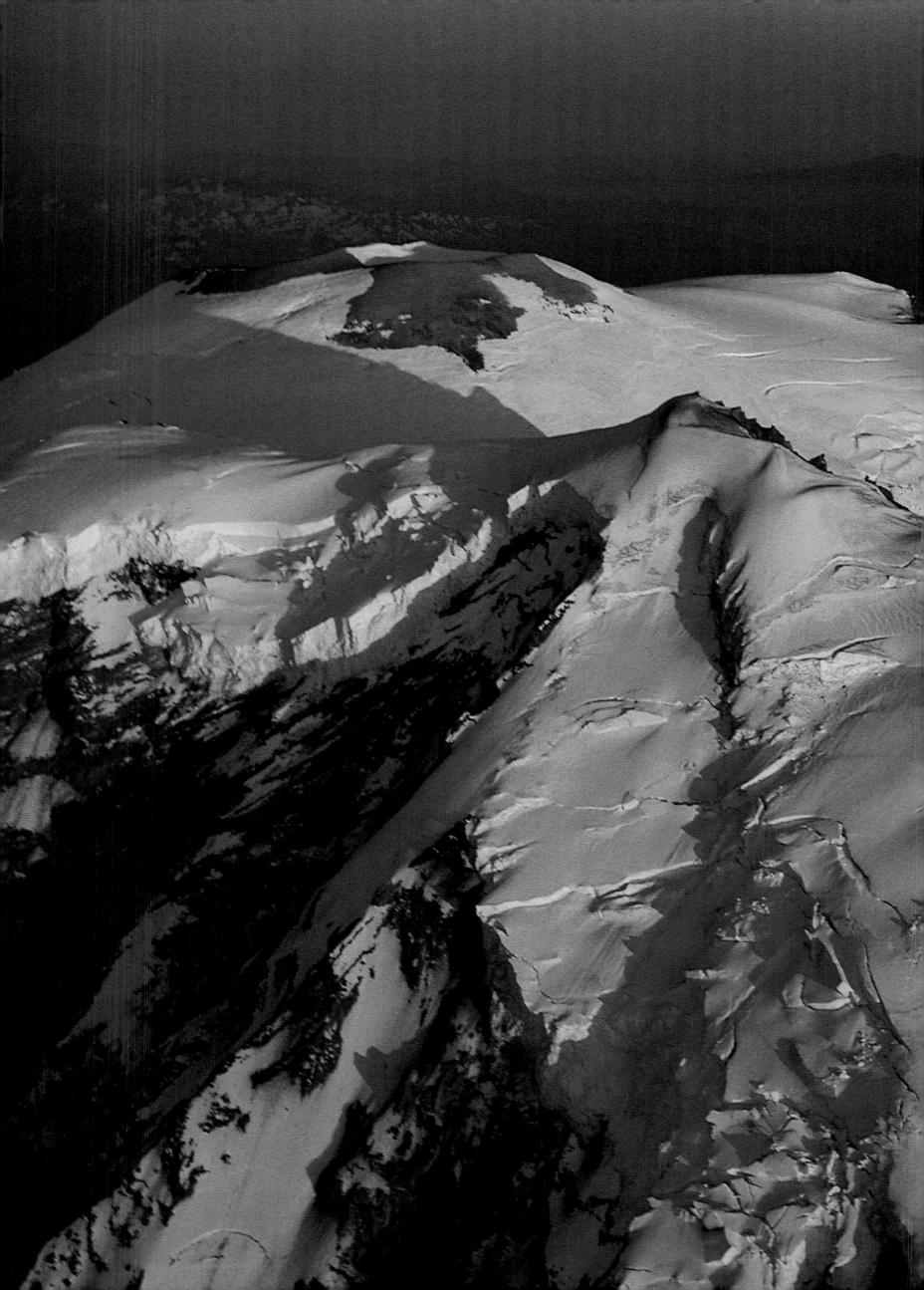

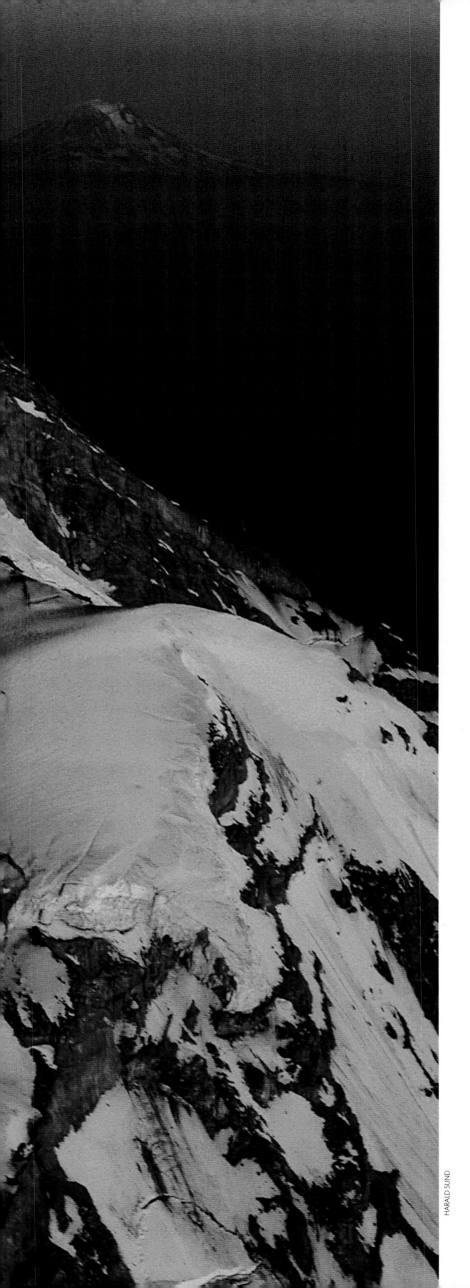

HARALD SUND

HARALD SUND

HARALD SUND

"*T*he eternal snows of ice-crowned Rainier" all but disappeared in the dry summer of 1988, but the crowning peak of the Cascades retained its grandeur and its status as Washington's prime tourist attraction. *Top:* Most visitors go no higher than Paradise Valley, 5,550 feet above sea level, aglow with alpine flowers in summer, buried under the deepest snow in the winter. *Above:* The architecture of the Visitors Center on the approach to Paradise is a reminder of the claimed first sighting of a flying saucer by a pilot flying over the shoulder of Mount Rainier.

227

HARALD SUND

*T*he tough conifers of the high slopes are
so designed by nature as to bear lightly
the heavy burden of snow.

*T*he Crystal Mountain resort just outside
Rainier National Park offers slopes for
active types who want to ski, and lodges
with fireplaces for those inclined to
"couch-potato" status.

The volcanos of the mountain playground are dormant, not dead, as Mount St. Helens so dramatically demonstrated. *Left:* Steam rises from the crater. The puffs to the right of Mount Adams are cumulus clouds.
Right: Looking east to west across the crater. *Below:* The forest blown flat by the eruption is preserved in the Mount St. Helens National Volcanic Monument, north of the summit.

THE RIVER

HARALD SUND

The dream of imports from Asia inspired the search for a Northwest Passage. Exports pay for imports. A grain-laden barge descends the Columbia carrying food for the people of the Pacific rim.

THE RIVER

"By whatever course may be taken from the Atlantic, the Columbia is the line of communication from the Pacific Ocean, pointed out by nature . . ."

Alexander Mackenzie, 1802

Previous pages

The Columbia sweeps beneath the Longview bridge toward the Pacific.

HARALD SUND

234

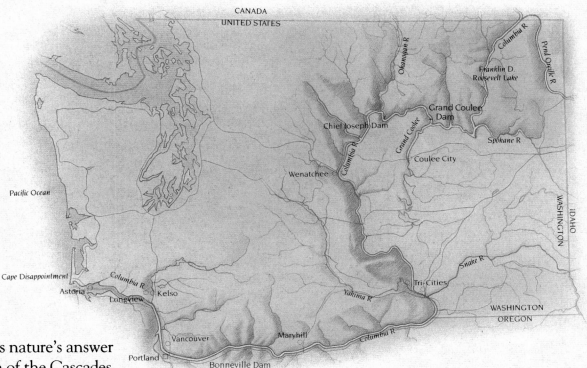

The Columbia is nature's answer to the problem of the Cascades. The river is the gravity route through the mountain barrier, the unifying path that links the wet side with the dry side.

The River of the West, the poet William Cullen Bryant's "Mighty Oregon," is Canadian at birth. It wells silent and unbubbled, six feet wide, from a stretch of gray glacial silt 2,619 feet above sea level in a valley cradled to the east by the Rockies and to the west by the serrated granite of the Selkirks. Banff lies only 80 miles to the northeast but on the far side of the Continental Divide. Eighty miles to the southwest is the invisible juncture of the borders of Idaho, Montana and British Columbia.

The water rising from the silt starts its 1,270-mile journey to the sea by flowing northwest. After its first mile it enters Columbia Lake, from which it emerges as a true river, but still slanting north by west on a course that would bring it to the Arctic Ocean in Alaska. After 230 miles (already longer than the Shenandoah or the Mohawk) confronted by the Cariboo Mountains, it makes a hairpin turn and follows the western slope of the Selkirks southward.

After travelling 500 miles, the Columbia is only 100 miles from its source. As it approaches the United States border, it absorbs the flow of the Clark Fork-Pend Oreille, which on its own 500-mile journey from Montana has gathered as much water as the River Colorado empties into the Gulf of California. Thus augmented, the Columbia crosses the 49th parallel to become American, and the captive of progress.

Once an untamed mustang, running free to the sea, the river now lies ponded behind dams—Grand Coulee, Chief Joseph, Rocky Reach, Rock Island, Wanapum, Priest Rapids, McNary, John Day, the Dalles and Bonneville—broken to harness, gentled, made useful.

Thirty miles below the border, the Canadian-born Kettle River joins it. In "olden" times—back in the 1930s—the meeting was a collision. The rivers shouldered each other into waves and whirlpools. Swirling currents pried boulders loose from the stream bed and enlarged the cavities into great potholes. The river plunged over two cliffs. French Canadian voyageurs of the Hudson's Bay Company called this bubbling stretch Le Chaudière (the cauldron). Today it is Kettle Falls, but the Falls are drowned now, a mere shadow in the depths of the 160-mile long Franklin D. Roosevelt Lake behind Grand Coulee Dam.

For Indians the disappearance of the Falls was another thread pulled from the fabric of their lives. For centuries tribes trekked annually to the rapids, each group allotted a few days to net and spear a year's supply of protein from the spawning run of the

Chinook salmon. The run began in mid-July and lasted two months. The Canadian artist Paul Kane, who painted the scene in September 1847, described it in his journal: "There is one continuous body of fish, more resembling a flock of birds than anything else in their extraordinary leap up the falls, beginning at sunrise and ceasing at the approach of night. The chief told me that he had taken as many as 1,700 salmon, weighing on average 30 pounds each, in the course of one day." The salmon come no more, nor do the Indians.

Just south of Kettle Falls, the Columbia is fed from the east by the gentle little Colville and, a hundred miles below the border, by the more powerful Spokane. Here too the going was once rough. A canoeist who shot the rapids at this juncture in the 1920s warned that "the agitated current [creates] breakers high and tempestuous." The risen waters of the Columbia have backed into the Spokane, and the streams now come together with no more commotion than two Dutch canals.

The Spokane seems to nudge the Columbia westward. It makes a sharp turn to the right as it encounters the edge of the congealed lake of basalt that underlies the arid central basin. For 300 miles no tributaries enter the Columbia River from the left, the land cupped in the Big Bend, the one-time desert that Grand Coulee Dam has brought to bloom.

Few pioneers crossing the Columbia Plain in the early days were tempted to take claims. Descriptive terms in journals and letters range from "dreary" and "dust-plagued" to "arid" and "this awfulness." A Scot called it "a desert, lacking even camels." In 1844 two British secret agents, dispatched during the "Fifty-four Forty or Fight" tension to see if the land was worth fighting for, saw nothing of value in the Big Bend: "The barrenness of the soil, the total absence of wood and water, completely excludes all hope of its ever being adopted to the wants of man."

Great Britain yielded the land below the 49th parallel to the Americans. Isaac Stevens, ever optimistic about the area he governed, praised the Columbia Plain he surveyed as "fertile, lacking only water." Critics did not fail to note the same could be said for hell. But Stevens was right about the soil. When a few farmers sowed wheat some years later, they rejoiced in harvests ranging from 25 to 50 bushels an acre. They planted more. The stored moisture of the covering bunch grass was exhausted. Deserted farmhouses, solid, windowless and gray, standing in fields where dust devils dance, are monuments to the folly of relying on unwatered soil.

Many would-be ranchers looked with the despair of Tantalus on the Columbia as it surged through the canyons it carved around the Big Bend. How could the life-giving flood be raised to the level of the farmlands? In 1918 an obscure county engineer suggested building a hydro-electric dam at a point below the Grand Coulee—the trough the river had carved during the ice age when diverted from its regular course. The dam could produce more than enough energy to pump water up into the Coulee, which could be dammed to serve as a reservoir supplying canals opening onto the arid acres of the lower Big Bend. A straightforward plan, massive . . . but simple. However, just as the desert lacked water, the plan lacked financing.

A country editor, Rufus Woods of the *Wenatchee World,* and a college professor, James O'Sullivan, were enthralled by the idea. They devoted 14 years to making County

Engineer C. W. Duncan's suggestion a reality. They were denounced as snake-oil salesmen. The president of the American Society of Civil Engineers described the proposed dam as "a grandiose project of no more usefulness than the pyramids of Egypt." *Collier's* magazine thought the Columbia Plain not worth saving: "dead land, bitter with alkali . . . even snakes and lizards shun it." The Coulee itself was written off as "a vast valley of rock and black wilderness inhabited by ghosts a hundred feet tall . . . The air you breathe is full of the dust of dead men's bones." As for the power that would be generated, who needed it? There would be enough unsold to light every prairie dog burrow in the Inland Empire.

The Great Depression and the Dust Bowl saved the day. Franklin D. Roosevelt came to the presidency pledged to create jobs. Whatever its other merits, building the world's largest artifact would require manpower. And with the soil of midwest farms blowing east with the wind, the creation of drought-proof farmlands out west made sense even in dusty New York. As for a surplus of power, there were jobs to be created. Congress authorized construction.

In the same way that bad times got the dam built, war time created uses for the extra energy. The first of Grand Coulee's giant generators—108,000-kilowatt units which dwarfed all others in the world—came on line on October 4, 1941, nine weeks before Pearl Harbor and three months before President Roosevelt set as a wartime goal the production of 50,000 airplanes a year. Planes required aluminum; the production of aluminum required power. Grand Coulee helped smelt the aluminum for the Flying Fortresses built in Seattle, ran the machines in the newly built shipyards on Puget Sound and the lower Columbia River, lit the barracks and the airfields. And there was energy left over for the vast secret enterprise that took shape on the sweep of sagebrush west of the meeting point of the Columbia and the Snake. Power from Grand Coulee helped the scientists and engineers to encapsulate the power of the atom in a plutonium bomb. The war ended with awful suddenness. New problems emerged slowly.

Power demanded power. The aluminum smelters absorbed the feared surplus of energy. More dams were built, a dozen in all on the Columbia and its tributaries. On the main stream, between the Canadian border and Bonneville Dam, where ocean tides begin to influence the river, only the stretch between Priest Rapids and McNary Dams remained unharnessed.

As new sources of hydro-electric power became scarce, Washington turned to nuclear energy. Ironically, it was at this point that the predicted power surplus developed. Nuclear power cost more than industry would pay. The Washington Public Power Supply System, in financial disarray, gave up on nuclear power. Then the federal government decided to end plutonium production at Hanford. The Tri-City area, where the small settlements of Richland, Pasco and Kennewick had exploded from hamlets into cities, faced a troubled period of reorientation.

What of agriculture? Not until 1953, 20 years after work started on Grand Coulee Dam, was a commercial harvest gathered from land irrigated by the project's reservoirs. But once started, the process continued. Other areas on the dry side are now watered by reservoirs supplied by the John Day and McNary Dams. All told, the Columbia brings water to 1,300,000 acres. Another 500,000 acres are fed by systems on smaller streams.

Sprinklers on a center-pivot system, motor-driven and water-propelled, have created a geometry of circular patterns as typical on the hills on the dry side as the rectangular outlines of clearcut logging are on the wet side of the mountains.

The dams downstream from the Tri-Cities not only produce power and provide water for irrigation but have so benefited river transportation that the inland cities of Kennewick, Pasco and Clarkston are now members of the Association of Washington Ports. Whereas once the residents of Washington longed for railroads to arrive to challenge the near monopoly on east-west commerce exercised by Oregon Steam Navigation (which controlled the portages between the rapids and thus the movement of bulk cargo), now grain producers welcome the competition that barge traffic brings to trains and trucks.

Gone, however, are the passenger steamers, which once offered travellers the luxury of hotel-like accommodation, unsurpassed scenery and the thrill of real danger. No longer can a visitor write, as did the German travel writer Theodor Kirchhoff in 1872: "The sole sign of civilization is our boat, snorting in her labors against the aqua-colored currents and therewith shuddering to her last seam. Smoke belches from her stacks. Sparks rain in a downpour on her upper deck. When she addresses one of many rapids, the drama is exciting. Between low, rocky shores she asserts her prow in the face of whirling, rushing water, now right, now left in short twists but ever ahead. Meantime the raging torrents appear to crowd her into the rocks while foaming waves lash her keel. The pilot steers with a steady hand through dangerous passages, faster here, slower there, feeling his way amid perils where the slightest carelessness will misguide beyond rescue. Sometimes the boat nearly stops in the sweeping flood and swings on her wide, powerful paddlewheel as if on a hinge, slowly, until the pilot's smart ring of the bell orders full steam ahead. Passengers generally watch this inspired navigation calmly, seeming to like nothing better than the most hazardous moments, when the boat escapes Charybdis only to encounter Scylla, and misses the treacherous rock by a hair."

The rapids now lie deep below the river surface. Winds funnelling downstream during the winter, upstream in summer and gusting up to 80 knots, have replaced rocks as the greatest hazard to navigation. Daredevils no longer run the rapids in canoes; they sail-board the waves above. What has not changed is the beauty of the Gorge, as handsome now as when the visiting Kirchhoff described the infrequent settlements as lacking the ambience of Bingen or Bonn but conceding that "the Columbia's aqua-tinted water is as beautiful as the Rhine's" and "not only equals but even exceeds the Rhine in majesty of rugged mountains."

Below the last dam, Bonneville (which was the first to be built), the water level is unchanged by man. Civilization intrudes but the topography is that described by the British who rowed up from their anchorage at the mouth of the river in 1792 and by Lewis and Clark who emerged from the Columbia Gorge in November of 1804.

The Corps of Engineers has made the Snake and Columbia
passable for barges in places where Lewis and Clark had to portage.
The Snake lies calm behind Lower Monumental Dam.

The Americans reported land "extending a great Distance to the right & left, rich [and] thickly covered with tall timber, with a few Small Prairies bordering on river . . . certainly a fertill and a hansom valley." After the arid interior, they welcomed the sight of "imense pine trees," but complained of being "kept awake during the whole of the night by the Swans, Geese, white and Grey Brant Ducks &c. They were emensely noumerous and their noise horid."

Carried by the waters gathered from a drainage basin of some 250,000 square miles, the canoes swept 80 miles in two days. On the morning of November 7, 1804, as they paddled through a lifting fog, the river ahead broadened dramatically: 'We are in *view* of the Ocian," Clark wrote that night, "This great Pacific Octean which we have been so long anxious to see, and the roreing or noise made by the waves brakeing on the rockey Shores (as I suppose) may be heard distinctly . . . Ocian in view! O! the joy."

The joy was premature. They were looking into Gray's Bay, not the Pacific. A southwesterly wind blew in off the ocean, pinning them for days in "a dismal nitch" on the Washington shore among "drift trees of emence size" that threatened to crush the canoes. When on November 15 the seas abated enough to allow them to round Ellice's Point and camp by an Indian village "uninhabited by anything except flees," they could at last see their goal—Cape Adams to the south, Cape Disappointment to the north, the breakers between and the true Pacific beyond, stretching to Asia.

Americans had reached the River of the West by land as well as by sea. A new relationship between the continents facing the Pacific was possible.

Previous pages ·

Below Bonneville Dam the river slows and broadens as it approaches the sea, but it is not always placid. Along this stretch the dugouts of the Lewis and Clark expedition were pinned for days, trapped among storm-tossed driftwood.

Chief Joseph of the Nez Perce said, "The white people would change the rivers if they did not suit them." The whites named this dam Chief Joseph.

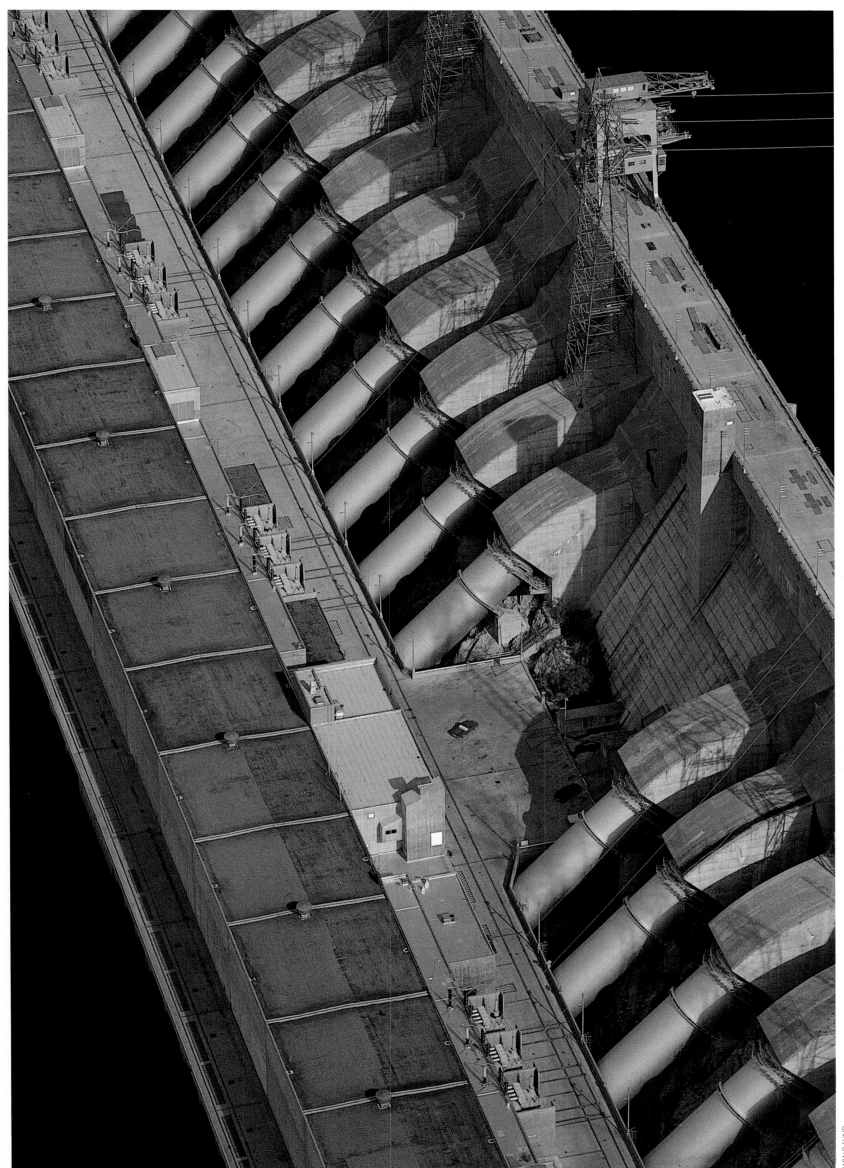

HARALD SUND

*T*he Pend Oreille, which rises in the United States, meets the Columbia, which rises in Canada, just north of the 49th parallel. The border is marked by the clearcut strip almost parallel to the road across the bottom of the picture.

HARALD SUND

*T*he Dry Falls of the Grand Coulee were carved, not over slow eons of geologic time but in a few days when an ice dam, holding back a great lake in Montana, gave way. The flood that swept across the Idaho panhandle and eastern Washington could have been seen with the naked eye from the moon.

As delicate as Grand Coulee is massive, the Tri-City bridge spans the Columbia near its junction with the Snake.

Locks such as this one at Ice Harbor Dam on the Snake have turned far-from-the-sea Lewiston and Clarkston into deepwater ports.

Grand Coulee Dam is one of the largest edifices built since the Great Wall of China. From lowest bedrock to the guardrail on top is 550 feet; from bank to bank, 4,173 feet. All the buildings in Rockefeller Center could stand on the 15-acre spillway with 3 acres left over.

HARALD SUND

Calmed by a series of dams, the Columbia stretches lake-like past Blalock Island toward Mount Hood on the horizon. The once-feared rapids slumber below.

For more than a century, wheat from the Inland Empire has poured into ships and barges for relay to downstream warehouses and elevators and to the markets of the world. This barge is passing a grain-loading facility just below the McNary Dam.

HARALD SUND

Sam Hill also commissioned the construction of a pseudo-Stonehenge, modeled on the one on the Salisbury Plain in Wiltshire, England. It is the scene of celebrations by the "Druids" of the New Age, at moments of mystic importance.

Sam Hill, who built the Peace Arch at the Canadian border, erected "Maryhill" as a family mansion but his family would not live in it. He wrote Loie Fuller, a Folies Bèrgère dancer, to say she had persuaded him to turn it into "a museum for the public good and the betterment of French art in the Far Northwest of America." Ten years later it was dedicated as an art museum.

HARALD SUND

*L*ongview, on the delta formed at the junction of the Cowlitz with the Columbia, was the site of an early settlement, which failed to prosper. In 1920 R. A. Long bought the area for a pre-planned lumber town. It did not develop as planned but still benefits from the surrounding timber.

*T*he setting sun turns the Columbia golden as it glides under the Interstate Bridge linking Vancouver and Portland.

HARALD SUND

*T*he Columbia estuary broadens into a
bay enclosed by jetties thrusting out from
Cape Adams and Cape Disappointment.
Beyond the bar lie the Pacific and the
markets of the world.

Index

THE PROJECT

Videographer Marc Pingry (left) and television director Jeff Gentes

To show Washington as it had never been before. To celebrate the state's centennial in a unique way. That was the goal when the project was first discussed with KCTS in 1987. Cameras rolling, we would traverse the state by fixed-wing airplanes and helicopters to capture the enormous diversity of the terrain and creativity and industry of its people. Out of this we would produce a pictorial and historical book of Washington from the air. KCTS planned a series of 36 short features to broadcast throughout the centennial year, culminating with an hour-long documentary airing November 11, 1989 — the official centennial of the state.

World-renowned photographer Harald Sund took to the air in December 1987 to begin his year-long odyssey for this book. The assignment was ideally suited to Harald, who specializes in landscape photography and who finds his home state is one of the most interesting corners of the world to photograph.

"It's not provincial to say that this is a great place in terms of the natural beauty the state holds," Sund said. "That is only confirmed when one looks at the state as a whole from the air. At 12,000 to 15,000 feet you can at once see Puget Sound, the length and breadth of the Cascades, the sunset over the ocean, the city lights, the ferries and ships, and the Olympics. I don't know of any other place on earth where you can do that."

Capturing the state from thousands of feet in the air proved easier than scheduling the shooting sessions themselves. Working off a "master list" of state events and locations, and expanding that list as events cropped up, Harald found he was able to cover 95 per cent of what he'd hoped to. "By September," he said, "the last pieces of the puzzle were put into place."

While Harald Sund was winging it through the state, Washington historian Murray Morgan was in front of his typewriter, recounting the past from a fresh point of view.

"Once I began writing, I found there was no way to tell all I could tell in 10,000 words," he said. "It was the first time I've written a book with so short a text. It was a real challenge and fun trying to figure out how to do it. I decided to use the text to describe what problems the land created for the first people who encountered it, and use the captions to indicate the way things have since developed."

The idea of focussing on how terrain affects the lives of the people on it intrigued Murray, who has possibly explored Washington's past from every conceivable angle in his numerous books and articles on the state. "Nobody has attempted a book of this kind before. Everyone will be able to see his home area from a different perspective."

Jeff Gentes, KCTS producer, saw that perspective first hand early on the project, as he joined videographer Marc Pingry in a vintage aircraft piloted by Rick Gerard.

"The video camera was mounted in protective housing on the nose of the twin-engine Cessna, automated from within the cabin by Marc," Jeff recalled. "The nose mount provided a stunning point of view perspective, with life rushing by at nearly 200 miles per hour. One must really have a stomach for aerial photography — such as when we'd bank into a steep dive over the North Cascades."

In the helicopter, the camera shot out of the side of the ship, mounted on a special device to insulate from the slicing rotor vibrations. The helicopter provided a tamer platform to work from, allowing the pilot, Glen Bell, to move it around objects in a gentle arc. More excitement was realized during some sequences, however, such as when the helicopter chased an agricultural spray plane across Walla Walla.

"In the flying business, pilots faithfully share a black sense of humor, which we all easily settled into, spiking our missions with a heightened sense of adventure," Jeff said. "Perhaps that is why, with the sun our lantern and Murray Morgan's words our inspiration, we would look down in awe over this extraordinary corner of earth called Washington and feel every bit like the early explorers who first captured its beauty."

The Underwriter

Seafirst is proud to be a sponsor of *Over Washington*. We believe this book and the accompanying KCTS television series are fitting tributes to what Washington has become in its first 100 years.

Since 1872, Seafirst has played a significant role in the economic growth of our state. However, our partnership with the people of Washington has only just begun.

In this centennial year, Washington is still on the frontier – a leader in aerospace, electronics, agriculture, retailing and other industries. Yet as these pages so dramatically illustrate, we are indeed fortunate that Washington also remains a place of astonishing natural beauty.

We hope you will enjoy this aerial celebration of our state. And we hope it will inspire you to meet more of the people and places of Washington in person. You'll find there really is no place like home.